RETIREMENT READY

HELEN WILLIAMS

RETIREMENT READY

What They Don't Teach You That You Need To Know

HELEN WILLIAMS

First published by Ultimate World Publishing 2020
Copyright © 2020 Helen Williams

ISBN

Paperback - 978-1-922372-28-4
Ebook - 978-1-922372-29-1

Helen Williams has asserted her right under the Copyright, Designs and Patents Act 1988 to be identified as the author of this work. The information in this book is based on the author's experiences and opinions. The publisher specifically disclaims responsibility for any adverse consequences, which may result from use of the information contained herein. Permission to use information has been sought by the author. Any breaches will be rectified in further editions of the book.

All rights reserved. No part of this publication may be reproduced, stored in or introduced into a retrieval system, or transmitted in any form, or by any means (electronic, mechanical, photocopying, recording or otherwise) without the prior written permission of the author. Any person who does any unauthorised act in relation to this publication may be liable to criminal prosecution and civil claims for damages. Enquiries should be made through the publisher.

Cover design: Ultimate World Publishing
Layout and typesetting: Ultimate World Publishing
Editor: Anita Saunders
Cover photo: simez78-Shutterstock.com

Ultimate World Publishing
Diamond Creek,
Victoria Australia 3089
www.writeabook.com.au

Disclaimer

Financial information provided in this publication is designed to be of a general nature only and does not represent professional advice. It is based on my own personal experience providing an overview and may not be applicable to every situation.

The ideas and strategies provided in this publication should not be used without first assessing your own personal and financial situation or without consulting a financial professional.

The author does not take responsibility for people applying the information inappropriately or failing to read and comprehend the information contained in this publication and will not be held liable for how the information is used.

To the maximum extent permitted by law, the author and publisher disclaim all responsibility and liability to any person, arising directly or indirectly from any person taking or not acting based on the information provided in this publication.

The author is not affiliated with and does not endorse any of the corporate entities mentioned in or involved in the distribution of this work or any third-party entities whose trademarks and logos appear in this publication.

Testimonials

Having known and worked alongside Helen for over 30 years, I have found that her extensive knowledge in the financial services industry has helped her set goals and objectives to enable her to achieve financial success and independence in both her professional and personal life.

For anyone striving for a strong financial future, I believe that if you are disciplined and follow the basic principles of Helen's book, you will go a long way to achieving your own goals and objectives.

Helen, congratulations on a fantastic book and I believe a lot of people will be helped and inspired by your work.

- Peter Toperosa, Financial Advisor,
Freedom Finance Australia

Having worked with Helen for three years, and been friends for 25 years, I have seen firsthand the enthusiasm and positive attitude she brings to whatever she tackles.

Her story demonstrates how an enthusiastic and positive attitude can help through adverse times. By using personal examples, she shows her advice is not theoretical but how it helps in a pragmatic way. Coupled with the knowledge and practical tips she has learned since getting her financial qualifications, her financial handbook is full of real-world examples on how to improve your financial future, and I encourage you to read it on your first step to a more secure financial future.

It has clearly worked for her, so why not for you?

- Clive Bayfield, Managing Partner,
Eastbourne Holdings LLC

Testimonials

I have known Helen all her life as our mothers have been friends since they were teenagers and are now in their mid-eighties.

Our lives have crossed paths many times over the years. I have always admired Helen's spirit, courage and determination to follow things through and make them happen.

Helen has always been very patient, ambitious, hardworking and when she sinks her teeth into a project, she follows it through to the nth degree.

Helen has hit some pretty big hurdles in her life both personally and professionally but has worked her way through them with true Aussie spirit and always kept her amazing sense of humour.

I've hit a few brick walls financially in my life and have turned to Helen for her invaluable advice.

It has been my pleasure to be a part of Helen's journey.

Helen's book and advice will be a turning point for so many people.

- Suzanne Lowe, Semi-Retired

Testimonials

I first met Helen over 10 years ago whilst she was temping with an organisation I was employed at. Our desks were next to each other and we hit it off instantly. I recall during one of our first conversations Helen said her goal was to retire early in a warmer climate than Melbourne. Well, she has achieved both and no doubt that is due to knowing exactly what she wanted and putting a plan/budget in place to achieve this.

Helen hasn't had a 'cruisy' life and has certainly encountered some very challenging times, both personally and professionally. It is amazing what can be achieved by having a plan, the power of positivity, resilience and perseverance—not to mention common sense, mingled with humour.

This book just makes sense. It is written in plain English, not financial jargon that most of us don't understand. It provides the tools to set you on your way to financial freedom—it's then up to you.

Many years ago during a development course with my then yoga teacher, the first piece of knowledge she imparted to the class was "If it is to be, it's up to me". I feel that this is exactly what Helen's book is saying with regards to your financial freedom. It's never too late to start.

Happy planning towards your financial freedom.

  - **Marie Farrugia, Personal Assistant at National Australia Bank (NAB)**

Testimonials

I met Helen over 10 years when she first joined NAB. From work colleagues we now have a great friendship based on trust and respect and have enjoyed many laughs and the odd tear along the way. Helen is my 'go-to' person and I value her counsel and advice. I have always admired Helen's determination, her desire to continue learning and her ability to take on extra work, and she can always find time to help someone along the way.

Helen, thank you for sharing your tips, goals and experiences. I wish I had this information when I was in my 40s but as you said, "It's never too late." I know this will help many women take control of their finances to assist in setting themselves up for life after work.

- Jill Gooding, Executive Assistant at Rabobank

I had the pleasure of meeting Helen several years ago when she purchased the unit next to mine.

At the time she was renting it out and planned to move into it, which she did in late 2019. One of her attributes is when she plans to do something, it's not just talk, she does it.

Helen impressed me with her many qualities that include but are not limited to ethical behaviour, business acumen, financial sense, and good old Aussie spirit and sense of humour.

Our strata title properties operate as a self-managed body corporate and I saw the opportunity to involve Helen. I recommended her for the chairperson and co-treasurer roles and she was voted in shortly after settling in late last year.

Testimonials

Since taking up official roles with our body corporate, Helen's contribution has been significant and she has improved our tendering process, followed up all issues and initiated our long-term maintenance program. All this has been achieved in a manner of respect and empathy.

Having read Helen's manuscript, what resonates with me is how her practical expression of what can seem complicated is written in common language. No super-technical speak, clichés or pie-in-the-sky concepts.

I have worked in the financial industry for over 10 years. Like Helen, if I had followed some simple principles as highlighted in her book, for example, debt consolidation, budgeting and knowing more about superannuation, I would have used my money to work harder for me, therefore, positioning myself better for a strong financial retirement.

I have been following Helen's concepts for several years since initially meeting her and I can now say that my financial position has improved as I do more with my income now than I did when I earned more money ten years ago.

Helen's book is a must-read for people to gain more control over their income and it's never too late to improve your financial situation.

Develop patience, persistence and perseverance and plan your steps.

- Ross F Kirby, Secretary and Treasurer of the Flame Tree Court Body Corporate

Contents

About the Author — xv
Acknowledgements — xix
Preface — xxi
Chapter 1: Flying Through Adversity — 1
Chapter 2: The Right Attitude, or the 3Ps — 13
Chapter 3: Setting Up for Success — 21
Chapter 4: The Ins and Outs — 31
Chapter 5: Personal Finance 101 — 47
Chapter 6: Superannuation—A Basic Introduction to Understanding Super — 63
Chapter 7: Building Your Nest Egg — 77
Chapter 8: The Common Denominator. It's YOU — 89
Chapter 9: Time to Take Control — 101
Chapter 10: Case Studies — 111

Resources
Offer 1: Free Budget Buster Template — 123
Offer 2: Bust Your Money Fears Complimentary Sessions — 124
Offer 3: Conference Speaking Services — 125

About the Author

Helen Williams left high school in 1973 and by January 2, 1974 was employed as a junior working for a Victorian hotel chain in Melbourne. She had no formal or tertiary qualifications, because back in those days of the early '70s, you basically had three choices of what to do with your life: go on to university and get a degree, get married or find a job, which is the option Helen chose.

Little did she know it would be the starting point of a career spanning over 47 years 'herding cats'. That's what she called it. If you want to put a title on it, Helen's been a personal assistant/executive assistant for over 40 years.

Over those years, Helen has worked across many industries including academia, aviation, architecture, pharmaceutical, not-for-profits, local and state government departments, and banking, just to name a few.

It was in the early '90s when the 'recession we had to have' kicked in and Helen was laid off as a result of that. She was devastated by the decision, as the job Helen was doing at the time was one of her favourites during her working life.

However, not to be deterred by what had happened, and because of her sheer determination, positive outlook on life and her 3Ps— Patience, Persistence and Perseverance—which have stood Helen in great stead all these years, she found employment again doing temporary assignments, which she loved.

During that whole time of the recession in 1990 – 1991, Helen was only out of work for one week. She tried her hand at anything that was offered to her and took it with enthusiasm and confidence. She learnt a lot about business and improved her skill sets with each new job.

By the mid-'90s, Helen decided that it was time to do something different, so she considered the idea of starting her own business and so Helen's Executive Secretarial Services was born.

Business was doing well. So well, that Helen took on the added responsibility of employing others to help her meet demand for the work she was being offered. You could say that Helen had created her own employment agency.

Along came 1995 and Helen, because of her own serious health problems diagnosed some 20 years earlier, again started another business after studying massage therapy for 18 months. This time it's about people's health and well-being and Health Wise Massage took off.

Helen's Executive Secretarial Services and Health Wise Massage were combined and MT&S Business Services was started. She worked five days a week for her secretarial business. Then she would come home, have her dinner and then go out and fulfil her massage appointments.

At the height of her massage career, which lasted 22 years, Helen had 50 clients and was working six nights a week. Something had to give and so she stopped her secretarial business and got work again this time working for an employer. But she loved these times.

About the Author

In 2012 and 2013, Helen was starting to feel concerned about people not knowing enough about their own financial well-being, so she completed her Diploma and Advanced Diploma of Financial Planning and was a Wealth Advisor for a bank working in a branch for some time.

In 2013, Helen won a national award for her Outstanding Contribution to the PA/EA profession, as voted by her peers.

Helen has done public speaking to the PA/EA world and spoken on topics of 'Having the Right Attitude' and project management and has mentored PA/EAs which again she simply loves.

Fast forward to now and Helen has done just about everything there is to do in someone's working life. Her pearls of wisdom are endless.

Her passion has always been to help others, to get things done and her 3Ps, which she lives by.

She believes that you need to make every post a winner and not hesitate to take a chance to do something if it comes your way or even speak up about it if you can see it on the horizon.

Acknowledgements

'Respect brings respect'. My parents have been a guiding light during my life and my father said this to me on the day I started my first job.

So, it's with heartfelt thanks to my parents, Heather and Les, who plucked me from obscurity amongst a nursery full of newborns, all those years ago. You have been on the journey with me through thick and thin.

And to a very special person who has been instrumental in allowing me to continue to work and enjoy life. It's a big thank you to this person and their family who gave me the chance for another crack at life. Without them making this sacrifice and gifting me their loved one's kidney, I may not have still been here to tell this story!

Preface

As the years pass faster and faster and with more uncertainty now more than ever, you need to take control of your finances right now.

This book is about the experiences I have encountered throughout my life and working career. It's about setting yourself up for success financially and will help women of all ages, although the examples shared will be of maximum benefit for those in their '40s, '50s and '60s that are heading towards retirement.

For many years now I've been concerned that as women we are not considering our own financial well-being and many of us when we get to thinking about retirement won't have enough money saved and will have a low superannuation balance on which to live by.

These are the reasons why I studied and got my qualifications in Financial Planning and along with my own experiences, it has given me extra knowledge which I want to share with everyone who reads this book.

It also worries me that women, particularly those who are renting and don't own their own home and are living by themselves, will be sure to face financial hardship as they stare down the face of retirement.

The statistics for women in their '50s and '60s here in Australia for homelessness because of their inadequate planning for retirement and financial health is suffering and I'm hoping that by writing this book women predominantly will start to do something about it.

It's never too late to take time out to consider and review your own financial health as you head into your '40s, '50s and '60s.

If you are a mum with teenagers, it won't hurt them to read it either as financial education is still a huge missing link in the high school curriculum. They may learn something from it as well and it could start them off on a path to financial literacy to help them in their adult life.

Lastly, the experiences mentioned in this book really occurred. They are my own personal experiences about my journey—where I've come from and what I'm doing now.

I hope you find this book to be interesting, inspirational, energetic and motivational.

It's time to get **Retirement Ready.**

Chapter 1: Flying Through Adversity

'Nobody said it would be easy, they just promised it would be worth it!'

It all started way back in the '70s, after replying to a job ad in the paper looking for an office junior, when I started working for Federal Hotels Limited, based at their head office up the top end of Swanston Street, Melbourne, opposite what is now RMIT (Royal Melbourne Institute of Technology). At the time, Federal Hotels had 32 properties in its hotel chain and they were scattered around Melbourne. Some in the CBD and others out in the suburbs. Places like Croydon, Bayswater, Essendon and St Kilda, to name a few.

I finished Year 11 at Glenroy High School in late December 1973 and by January 2, 1974 I was employed full time. Wow, my first job. It was a role for a person straight from school like myself, with no qualifications whatsoever, and it encompassed all sorts of daily tasks. I would sort and distribute the mail, make teas and coffees for the senior executives, run errands (not the courier companies around then like there is today), do the filing and generally any other task that no-one else wanted to do. I really enjoyed it. I was always busy and learnt lots and got to meet heaps of people from all levels of the business. I was so excited to be out in the workforce and to be paid for what I was doing.

Sixty dollars was my first pay packet. It was made up of cash and included a slip of paper with my name and address on it, my hours worked and total amount paid inside a gold Kraft envelope (for those of you who don't know what a gold Kraft envelope is, examples on the next page).

I couldn't wait to go shopping. I've always had a love for retail therapy. Didn't take me long to spend it all except for $10 which I gave to my mother for board. I can remember spending it in Katies. Yes, Katies. They used to have a massive store in Bourke Street (where the mall is now). I thought it was Christmas.

However, in 1978 during the early years of my marriage, something changed my life. It wasn't a job, it wasn't technology. It was my health.

I was diagnosed with chronic reflux nephritis. Or in layman's terms, I had a form of kidney disease. Only mine was more serious and life threatening. This certainly had put paid to having a family and I would endure treatment for some time. But I pushed on regardless, trying to never worry about things as stress was one of the worst things for progressing the disease.

In 1982, Taverns of Victoria took over the Federal Hotels and I was promoted to the position of executive secretary/office manager for the group. In this capacity, I was responsible for organising the program for the general manager and his six senior executives which included attending to all typing and filing. Typing by the way wasn't on a laptop, but an electric

Chapter 1: Flying Through Adversity

IBM golf ball typewriter. I also did all the travel arrangements, coordinated all appointments/meetings, organised functions and attended events.

IBM Selectric (Golf Ball) Typewriter

By 1985, 11 years later, I'd advanced through the company performing various roles as they were offered to me. I'd moved my career path from that of an office junior to PA (personal assistant), or as we were known back then, executive secretary.

At the time, there wasn't much more to learn within the business which I loved, unless I branched out to become an assistant manager in one of the hotels and I wasn't interested in that. I was married and had no wish to do night shift or weekend work, so finally after some hesitation I left the hospitality industry and the people that I had grown up with to take some time out and travel overseas. It was time for me to see the world.

Travelling throughout Europe and beyond for six months, I used the skills I had gained from doing all those travel bookings and relished seeing the different cultures, people, places and everything else that travelling abroad offers.

I came back to Melbourne and it wasn't long before I was offered a temp assignment working in academia. La Trobe University, in fact, although it was known then as Lincoln School of Health Sciences. I was a senior secretary working for the School of Health Administration and Education. Wow, just so different to what I had left back in the hospitality industry.

Duties included all the usual tasks that I had performed when I was the executive secretary/office manager for Taverns of Victoria.

Only now office technology was changing and gone were the IBM electric golf ball typewriters. What was known as the IBM Displaywriter was introduced into the office environment and this was my first foray into computers. Still not as we know them now. Rather big and clunky and took up most of your desk. But it changed the way we, as secretaries, typed. Didn't have to worry about changing golf balls to get different type fonts or using carbon paper to do numerous copies. It was faster and more reliable.

No Liquid Paper, or Tipp-ex, as we called it, to wipe out any typing errors you may have made.

Chapter 1: Flying Through Adversity

IBM Displaywriter (Courtesy of DigiBarn Computer Museum and IBM)

What was meant to be a temp assignment for only a few weeks went on to become a permanent full-time position and I was now working for the School of Orthoptics.

That was 1986 and life was turned upside down again when my marriage of 10 years finally came to an end. There were no hard feelings and it was a very amicable divorce. Thankfully my husband at the time was very considerate about dividing up the assets as to who got what, etc., and I managed to come through the divorce emotionally, physically and financially okay.

Although now, not only do I have a serious kidney complaint, I'm newly divorced and in a new job. I'm a 29-year-old female and starting from scratch again.

It was by this time, I thought to myself, *Helen, you need to write down one personal goal and work hard to achieve it*. I wrote that I wanted to be a millionaire and I knew the only way I was going to achieve that was to get started investing in properties. It wasn't going to happen overnight but with time and planning it was achievable. I saved as much or as little as I could.

Then two years on came some great news. I was fortunate enough to receive a kidney transplant on June 7, 1988. Wow, this was life changing for me. I had been having treatment for about 10 years when I received a message on my pager that a kidney was available for me and that I needed to admit myself to hospital asap for the life-saving operation. It certainly came at the best time as I was getting sicker and had lost so much weight I was turning green and weighed 47 kilograms.

Still in full-time employment with La Trobe and with a new kidney, I studied for my marketing qualifications and after four years in academia, in 1990 I decided to leave and took up a role as a sales support/secretary role with a drawing office supplies company, Aarque.

Back in those days, any sort of document which involved drawing, such as plans for houses, etc., were hand drawn. No CAD in those days. And so, this was totally different again to where I had just come from and I loved it. Think I might have been born into sales as I do have the gift of the gab.

Unfortunately, by November of that year, I was put off, or made redundant, as they say today, because of "the recession we had to have", the famous words from Paul Keating, the then-treasurer.

Chapter 1: Flying Through Adversity

It's the end of 1990 and now two years on from receiving my kidney transplant and raring to go, I launched my own business, Helen's Executive Secretarial Services. For 10 years, I 'herded cats' in personal/executive assistant roles for Avis Car Leasing, a private architectural firm, Symbol Australia, Comcater-CCE, Grundig Dictating Company, Department of Human Services, Utilities Insurance, Moreland City Council, Kraft Foods and lastly Anglican Aged Care.

And because of my prior health issues, I knew what it meant to have good health, and so I studied both relaxation massage and sports massage in 1993/1994. I wanted to help people with their aches and pains, with their stresses of everyday life, and massage certainly did that. So, in 1995 I launched Health Wise Massage. For 22 years I massaged my clientele of 50 people from all walks of life, even more so going out of my comfort zone and did it by way of home visits. I massaged six nights a week and by day, I tended to my secretarial clients. You could say I was a busy girl.

Some might say I was a pioneer in some respects as I also mixed my business with various temp assignments along the way, in what is known today as having a 'side hustle'. I also employed two other people to help me out when I had my contract with the Department of Human Services. My own employment agency, you could say.

January 1995 also saw the fruits of my labour come to fruition. Each year I continued to write down my personal goal of wanting to be a millionaire. Well, the time had come. I'd saved enough for a deposit. Nothing too grand. Just needed to get my foot in the door, so to speak. Nice two-bedroom unit in Williamstown, Melbourne. Not too far from the beach. At last I had my first investment property, but the goal was still there for me to achieve.

I decided to give up being self-employed after about 10 years when I landed a dream job with Ansett Australia.

Looking back at my involvement in the Australian aviation industry at a time of development and turmoil, it was an exciting time. I had a fascinating job with great people and prospects, plus the chance to travel. But almost 12 months later my dream job turned into a nightmare.

It was the day after the September 11, 2001 attack on the twin towers of the New York World Trade Centre by hijacked passenger aircraft that my job with Ansett came to an end. The airline collapsed as suddenly and as surely as the twin towers and within two days Ansett's fleet was grounded.

I thought at last I had found my niche in my working life and through no fault of my own it came tumbling down. However, I emerged from the Ansett wreckage with resilience and my enthusiasm intact.

I got through all of this using what I call the three Ps—persistence, patience and perseverance. They helped me get the job with Ansett, just as they helped me through the collapse of my marriage, my health and getting back on track with my career.

From Ansett, I moved on to another role; by now it's 2001 and I'm ready to look for my next investment property, moving ever so closer to my personal goal that I was working towards for my retirement. I knew I would never be able to save a million dollars but if I could accumulate my wealth through property investment, by the time I was ready to give up work and retire, even semi-retire, with that million dollars, there was my superannuation. A lovely sum of money that used wisely and correctly would enable me to lead a comfortable lifestyle.

So, after much research and Melbourne getting more and more expensive, I decided to look at properties in Queensland. The market was cheaper up there and so was stamp duty. Next thing I knew I was the proud owner of a two-bedroom unit in Mooloolaba on the Sunshine Coast. I was edging closer to my personal goal.

September 2003 and after completing a two-year contract with TXU, a utilities company, I took an executive assistant position with CSL, a pharmaceutical company. It was one of my most satisfying roles. I would stay at CSL for five years. Not only was it then that I realised I was always going to be a career PA, but I had also managed to pay off my first investment property in Melbourne. Time to celebrate! I was slowly but surely getting closer to that magical figure, one million dollars.

At this stage, I'm now 52 years of age, one investment property paid for, and another one sorted. It's now that I'm thinking more seriously of my retirement plan. My focus on my 3Ps kicks into gear again when I decide to leave CSL and pursue other roles.

Finally, in June of 2009, I enter the banking world and accept a PA role with NAB. Again, it's so different from pharmaceuticals, but I have a thirst for knowledge and love learning new skills and it's not long and I've got my boss organised and I'm working well with him and his leadership team.

Fast forward nine years and in April 2018, NAB was looking at how it could streamline its business and so there was an opportunity for me to take a package, which I accepted.

Oh, by the way, by now my Mooloolaba property has been paid off and it was in March 2011 that I bought property investment number three in Redcliffe, Queensland. Another two-bedroom unit about 600 metres from the beach and local shopping strip. About 35 minutes north of Brisbane.

At last, I have reached my personal goal. It's taken me all those years; however, it certainly has been worth it. My property investments are worth over a million dollars. One point two million dollars, in fact.

But I'm too young to retire and so I accept a contract role with Tiger Airlines and I know that having my previous experience all those years ago with Ansett got me over the line. It's a contract role with a PA title, free car parking and only eight minutes from home. I couldn't ask for any more.

I'm in great shape now to plan what I want to do without having to worry too much that I won't have enough in my super to live off when I finally decide to call it quits.

Again, my 3Ps kick in and I decide that's it. March 2019 and I finally say, 'enough is enough'. After 'herding cats' for 45 years, it's time to reflect and plan my life now for going forward. I have managed to save well over the years and I have my investment properties.

So, I started working on boosting my superannuation balance. Like most women, I didn't have a huge amount in super. In

Chapter 1: Flying Through Adversity

fact, when you read the chapter on superannuation, I didn't have much over $115,000. I had slightly more than the average because I decided I didn't want to be one of the statistics and so I did what is called 'salary sacrificing'. More on that in Chapter 7.

July 2019, I sold my Mooloolaba property for about three times the price I paid for it. I added a significant portion from the sale of the property to my super. It was now looking somewhat healthier. I also put some into my savings and kept an amount separate to pay for the capital gains tax I would have to pay later that year. I still have my investment property in Williamstown, Melbourne and that is providing me some income until I finally decide to sell it and add more to my super.

Fast forward to January 2020. I've been in a lot of paddocks and things are not necessarily greener on the other side.

But it was my Ansett experience in which I turned adversity on its head and the 3Ps, my mantra in life which has helped define me and who I am.

Before I finish this chapter, I want you to do one thing for me and yourself. Sit down and write down one personal goal. It must be SMART! Specific, measurable, achievable, relevant and timely. It can be anything. Mine was to be a millionaire and I achieved that through hard work, saving and getting into the property market to accumulate my wealth.

I also want you to have 3Ps in your life. They could be the same as mine. Patience, persistence and perseverance. It could be patience, people, passion. They're out there. You just need to take some time out to reflect what they are for you and then live by them. Both in your personal life and your professional life.

Lastly, don't be frightened of change. Most people are fearful of change. Look for the positives of change, not the negatives, and always feel free to pick up the phone and call me. I'm always here to help you to 'brainstorm' or bounce ideas off.

I believe in karma … that things happen for a reason. So, hang in there and let them happen!

Chapter 2: The Right Attitude, or the 3Ps

'Don't lose hope; when the sun goes down, the stars come out.'

From the day I started working, I knew that if I wanted to get anywhere in business, and in life for that matter, I needed to have a positive attitude.

Having a good, positive attitude, along with positive thinking at work will reflect on what I can do and makes me a more productive person. It determines how well I get my daily tasks done and how others perceive me. If you display the right attitude, one that is positive and productive, you may increase your chances for a promotion or a raise if you are a positive role model for others within your department at work.

As I say, your attitude determines your altitude. Attitudes are defined as established ways of responding to people and situations that we have learned, based on our beliefs, values and assumptions we hold. Attitudes can manifest through your behaviours. It is your attitude that determines how fast you achieve your goal or how well you acquire a skill or knowledge.

Attitudes also provide a framework to solve the problem. Attitudes drive behaviour. If you want to succeed at anything you need to have the right mindset. Almost always, you have a choice as to what attitude to adopt. If you feel angry about something that happens, for instance, that's how you choose to feel. It is your choice. And since you have a choice, most of the time you'll be better off if you choose to react in a positive rather than negative way.

What's the Significance of Having the Right Attitude?

Your attitude is a form of an expression of yourself. You can choose to be happy, positive and optimistic or you can choose to be a pessimist and critical with a negative outlook on your workday or your life in general. Taken from some research I read about years ago about having a good attitude at work, it 'suggests that positive thinking and a good attitude helps your psychological well-being and helps you cope better under stressful situations at work'. Therefore, if you display a good attitude, your co-workers will as well, making it easier to communicate and get along in the workplace.

This is also relevant to each of us in our daily lives. It doesn't help if one partner has had a bad day at work and then brings home all that pent-up frustration, anxiety, etc. The other partner gets the 'bad vibes' and often in the end feels the same way. With someone coming home after work or whatever the case may be, it's going to be less stressful and more beneficial for your health if you are feeling positive and good about things. Sure, you might have problems; however, what's important is that by being calm and positive you will certainly be better at listening to each other's concerns and be able to cope with the situation. Makes for a much happier life when each person can talk to each other calmly and rationally.

The Benefits of Such

When you begin to display a positive attitude at work and with your life, you can expect to see benefits. If you must make a presentation or share a project with others at work, keep your

Chapter 2: The Right Attitude, or the 3Ps

attitude upbeat and hopeful for a positive outcome. Reinforce with others the rewards of your goals and emphasise less on the negatives. This will keep other employees, including yourself, motivated and on track. Same goes when dealing with a relationship.

It Helps the Atmosphere of Your Work Environment

Your attitude is the first thing people pick up on in face-to-face communications, i.e. job interviews. Just as laughing, yawning and crying are infectious, so too is your attitude. Before you say a word, your attitude can infect the people who see you with the same behaviour.

Somehow just by looking or feeling, you can be infected by another person's attitude, and vice versa. I know myself that there have been times when I've been feeling fantastic and when I've spoken to people, they tell me that they feel inspired by the conversation that I have had with them. However, it can be trying for you to have a good attitude in the workplace when the atmosphere is negative or other employees are unhappy. You can suggest ways to increase morale to your boss.

In one PA role that I was involved in, it was as simple as having a morning or afternoon tea for team members' birthdays. This sort of thing had not been done before and it was a way of bringing the team together on a more informal footing. For the rest of the team it provided some necessary bonding as generally the team members kept to themselves.

Or it could be inviting a motivational speaker along to one of your team or department meetings. The key is to change the tone in the office to a positive and uplifting one. This also helps to induce productivity and makes employees feel as if they are wanted and part of the team.

The Effects of Such

When you expect positive outcomes, you can turn a bad circumstance into a new opportunity. This gives you a chance to learn from your experience and investigate new ideas on how to make the next project or activity a more beneficial one. Reacting with an attitude that you can learn from the negative rather than give up or get mad will show that you are a team player and someone who can bounce back from stress.

By having the right attitude and approach to my work and fellow employees and my life in general, I'm certain that had it not been for my enthusiasm to learn more and willingness to adopt a positive approach and outlook on my work, I probably wouldn't be where I am now.

Identification of a Good Attitude and Approach

There are signs of a good attitude and these signs are identified by employers and management, who look for leaders in a group or those to whom they want to give projects to. Those employees who are committed to volunteering some of their extra time and are appreciative, enthusiastic, kind and willing to help others with a good attitude are often recognised in the workplace.

I believe that too many of us just look at the small picture; that is, we just go about doing our normal, mundane tasks at work and with our lives daily. You need to be aware of the bigger picture and how by streamlining your position at work, you will be able to add value to not only your working environment but the rigours of life.

What Are My Practical Tips You Need to Excel at Being a Positive Person?

Well, I've always believed that an effective person is one who has the following qualities: patience, persistence and perseverance—these three qualities have stood me in good stead all my working life and so I call them my 3Ps. Without them I wouldn't be where I am now because there has been the occasional situation where I could have easily thrown in the towel when things weren't working out for me or going my way and so it's only by living by my 3Ps that I have managed to shape the career and life that I have.

People and passion also play an important part in being a positive person. If you can't get on with the people you work alongside of and those that you deal with externally, then you may as well go and do something else. As for passion, it's known that when a person is passionate about their occupation, they find it less work and more rewarding, get more done and are more satisfied. In other words, when people generally enjoy their profession, they are usually more motivated and driven to succeed in what they do and are happy and satisfied doing it.

I would like to say that if you have these traits and the right positive attitude or mindset, call it what you like, I'm sure you will continue to enjoy your time as a positive person at work, as a successful business owner, if that's what you are intending to aspire to, as everything else will just fit into place for you.

Remember, your attitude affects everyone, even yourself. You can't do anything to change the fact that a problem exists; however, you can do a great deal to find the opportunity within that problem. You're guaranteed a better tomorrow by doing your best daily and developing a plan of action for the tomorrows that lie ahead.

Just remember to maintain a positive mental attitude so that, as you plan for tomorrow, you're doing so with the sense of expectancy that produces substantially better results.

You can achieve everything you have ever wanted to have, experience or become. The power has and always will be within you; however, nothing will happen until you get and stay motivated to make something happen, to change your life and achieve your desires.

This is a lesson I learnt several years ago when I moved from being a personal assistant to a wealth advisor. It was up to me to change the way I felt about being a personal assistant. I wanted a change after all those years and so I decided to use the financial qualifications I had gained and get a role as a wealth advisor as I was keen to help people with their financial well-being. Only it didn't work out and so by using my 3Ps (patience, persistence and perseverance) as I had done on several occasions in the past, I realised it was time to get out of the negative rut that I was in doing this role, and so I decided to get back into the PA world once again, still with NAB.

Chapter 2: The Right Attitude, or the 3Ps

And so, it was with a positive attitude and the right approach that I dug deep within myself and I again took a situation and turned it into an opportunity. Eventually I was back doing a PA role up until my role was made redundant at NAB and I was paid out. I went on from there to another full-time contract role with Tigerair and then resigned to get my virtual assistant business up and running.

I set up my VA business a couple of years ago now as I wasn't exactly sure what I wanted to do. I knew that I didn't want to work full time at being an employee anymore. By now I was in my early 60s and had been 'herding cats' for over 45 years. I'd set my life up that I didn't need to work full time. By getting my VA business off the ground, it gave me freedom to work with whom I wanted to, the hours I wanted to work, I could choose what type of work I wanted to do, I could work from home or wherever, could earn reasonably good income and still have time in my life to do other things during the week rather than on the weekend.

However, while there were several positives, there was a negative aspect to it as well. When working from home or remotely, I didn't interact with other people until I went out and met with people. Unlike being in an office all the time. And I found this a bit frustrating as I'm a people person and like contact with others.

It's only now because of a more agile, flexible workforce, it's become a more common way of working. Terrific if you are a mother of young children and want to work from home. You can drop them off to school, go home and head off into your little office that you have created, work for several hours, go and pick them up from school, etc.

Fast forward to November 2019 and after many years of wanting to move to Queensland—I was born in Melbourne and have lived there all my life—I finally did just that. My three Ps—patience, persistence and perseverance—once again played an important role in my decision to make the move.

February 2020 and I'm now living out a dream that I knew one day would come to fruition. Living by my three Ps and my positive attitude, I'm doing what I want, when I want.

This is also possible thanks to myself thinking about my financial well-being as I approached my 50s. With no children to take care of me and/or partner for that matter to help me out if a situation arose, I wanted to be in the position that I could live out my '60s, '70s and maybe '80s without too much stress in my life. I didn't want to worry about where I was going to find my next dollar to pay for my rent or bills. I knew that if I planned my life to be in great shape financially that I would be okay, and it's come from hard work, thinking smartly and learning all the time.

After all, your financial security is dependent on your attitudes and beliefs about money and your willingness to take your financial future into your own hands!

All this brings me back to what I believe is having the right attitude: towards people, the next role job interview, whatever it might be …

Chapter 3: Setting Up for Success

'Nothing is impossible, only miracles take a bit longer'—Helen Williams.

Why It Pays to Have a Plan

There is no better time to set and manage your financial plan and come out on top than at the start of each financial year which runs from July 1 each year to June 30 the following year. A fresh look at your spending, direct debits, comparing your insurances, for example, could bring about some surprise savings for you and set you up for success.

Here's how to get started:

Map Out Your Goals

The first step in your planning is figuring out what you really want to achieve financially in the next year or even five years. You need to start with a short-term goal, as well as considering having long-term goals, and it's good to get them in line.

Think of a goal as a destination. If the goal is not clear, it is difficult to get to that destination. In order to plan properly, a clear distinction between short-term and long-term goals is essential. To help differentiate between these two terms, here are their differences.

I consider a short-term goal is generally something that is going to happen in the next 12 months. For example, this could be a holiday.

A long-term goal, on the other hand, is an outcome that you want to accomplish in the future. Long-term goals are not something that you can do this week or even this year. It is usually at least several years away before your long-term goal is fulfilled, particularly when you are considering financial goals.

Some hints for creating a winning goal:

Get Specific

I started up a separate bank account years ago and called it my travel fund and each week I put a certain amount of money in it and it was used to pay for a trip that I would take each year. This was a short-term goal. I never had to worry about coming back from my trip and thinking how on earth I was going to pay for it. And I didn't have to dabble into my savings either. It was always a holiday that I could enjoy, and I could relax, not having to worry about what it was costing me.

To this day, I still put a certain amount of money aside in my travel fund each week and I know it's there for a holiday whenever I want to go somewhere to relax, explore new places or meet new people. A no-stress holiday. I even have the money to take out travel insurance and spending money. Everything is covered.

Once I put in place my first long-term goal of wanting to be a millionaire, my next long-term goal was to pay off my mortgages for my investment properties sooner than the 30 years that they were taken out for. I set myself a goal that I would have each one paid off in 15 years. I did this by putting aside more money

Chapter 3: Setting Up for Success

each week to put on my mortgage to reduce it more quickly. Even when I was married back in the '70s, each week an extra $10 was put towards the mortgage and we decided to also make our repayments fortnightly. This was also back in the days when interest rates on mortgages were between 9.13% and 17%. Nothing like the rate in 2020 of 0.50%. I can remember paying 14% on our mortgage at one stage and thinking to myself that we would never pay off our house.

In the mid-'80s I got divorced, and although our loan balance was $10,000 at the time, we had managed to pay off $18,000 in 10 years of marriage from a total of $28,000 just by planning and setting our goals. Had we stayed married our goal of paying off the mortgage in 20 years would have been well and truly accomplished. It's all relative.

Put Pen to Paper

Don't be frightened to pick up a piece of paper and a pen and sit down and play with some figures to get a feel for setting your goals. Putting your goals in writing means they are not just talk. Writing several goals down can help you focus on which ones mean the most to you.

Be Realistic

Goals are dreams that are doable, so make sure that you can make your goals a reality and put aside the amounts you need to make each goal possible and achievable.

I would often grab a blank piece of paper and work on all sorts of figures. Working out 'what if this situation' or 'what would happen if' most times to crunch some numbers and to give me peace of mind. A big part of the planning and goal-setting process goes hand in hand with budgeting.

Make sure your goals are measurable. By that I mean whatever goal it is you have written down on your plan, you need to keep monitoring your progress. How close are you to meeting your goal? How much do you need to save?

Goals should also come with a deadline or an end date. Ask yourself how long it will take you to accomplish your goal. Working within a time frame allows you to better track your progress.

For me, I started with my first goal to be achievable in 10+ years. That's when I wanted to be a millionaire. From there, I broke it down into smaller goals with different timelines that I knew were attainable and relevant to my life and were meaningful to me. I knew that I wasn't going to have a huge amount in my superannuation account to live comfortably on as I neared my 60s, so I started planning in my 40s and finally, all these years on, I've got there.

Master Your Spending

Next, it's time to look at your spending patterns or habits. Let's be realistic, spending money is all part of enjoying life; however, a few small changes here and there could get your money working harder for you.

I've always been frugal with my money which means that I have saved for this and that, put funds aside for a travel account,

Chapter 3: Setting Up for Success

paid more off my investment properties or whatever; I still, to this day, love my retail therapy.

I'm not frightened to spend my money when I know that I can afford to. No matter what you're shopping for, you can usually find sales, discounts and deals, so it's smart to take advantage of them whenever they occur and you are looking to buy something. Why would you pay full price when you can get it cheaper when it is on sale?

However, they're there to make you want to shop, so be a savvy shopper rather than an impulsive shopper, getting sucked in by the sales. Only buy if you can afford it, even at sale price.

Some other simple ways to save are:

- Doing your food shopping in the evening, as sales and discounts are often available towards the end of the day
- Waiting until 2 p.m. to nip out for lunch; not only do you not get caught in the rush, you may find discounts on certain foods like sandwiches or salads. I know I have done this in the past and what was full price at midday is now reduced by a couple of dollars
- Organising catch-ups earlier in the week, as many restaurants and cinemas offer cheaper deals or tickets earlier in the week
- Finding the best price to fill up on petrol. There are apps out there that can help you find the location of where petrol is being sold cheaper than at other places. Even getting cheaper petrol with your supermarket reward cards

- Keeping an eye out for coupons that may appear in your letterbox or on your phone apps. These are a great way to enjoy life's little pleasures without the full price tag.

If you were to grab that piece of paper and write down every time you filled up at the service station and how much you saved for the year, I'm sure it would be a significant amount and you're not even realising this.

Also, as mentioned earlier, I love to travel so when the website Luxury Escapes came along, I thought *wow, this is a great way to have a holiday with all the luxuries for less.* I've since done a few Luxury Escape packages and I've never been disappointed. Not only have I saved money on each trip, I've also had more money left in my trip account which I leave in readiness for my next adventure, whenever that may be.

Delve Into Your Direct Debts

How often do you use your gym membership? Could you be doubling up on Netflix costs in your household? These are important questions you need to consider because there could be savings hidden in your old direct debits.

Have a think about:

1. Your gym membership: have you been putting off going for a while? It may be time to swap your cross trainer for the great outdoors and put the membership on hold.

2. Your phone bill: have you been on the same contract for over a year? It might be time to negotiate a new deal for your loyalty.

3. Your subscriptions: it can be easy to accumulate these, but they all add up. You can make simple savings just by streamlining your subscriptions.

4. Your bills: while paying by direct debit can help you unlock early payment discounts, make sure that you cancel any direct debits that you no longer need.

5. Lastly, and this is a biggie: compare your insurance costs. Again, there are apps available to help you compare your health, home and car insurances to make sure that you are getting the best deal possible.

Prepare for What's Ahead

Once you have freed up some cash with your spending, you can start to build your savings. Setting a savings goal each month that you can afford is a great start and whatever you do try not to dip back into it once it's set aside.

As I didn't go anywhere last year, I know that my travel fund is still building up each week so when my trip to Perth eventuates this April, I will have more than enough in my account to cover this and still plenty there for what lies ahead.

Back in the early days, I had an account which was my Christmas Club account and I put a certain amount of money into that each week as well which meant that at Christmas time, I didn't have to use my savings. This was before the days of credit cards.

If, like me, you have several different goals for next year, and I'm hoping you have, otherwise this has all been pointless, you can set up several different accounts like I did and still do. You can even name them in the apps available after your goals, so you can see immediately that safari getting a little closer each month.

Or you can keep it very simple like I did when I was married; I had what I called a 'bill jar' and it was an old jam jar that I hid in the kitchen that I would put a designated amount of money in each week. As the bills came along, I would use this money to pay them. Again, not having to dip into my savings.

Build an Emergency Fund

To be prepared just in case of a little emergency, you could aim to set aside a rainy-day fund and keep your savings safe from any surprise setbacks in the future. One just never knows what's around the corner, so best be prepared for all situations.

Having a fund that contains a build-up of cash that will cover six to nine months of expenses if you are operating on a single income or three to six months if you're in a two-income household will help you out if times get tough, such as an illness, job loss or an unexpected home or car repair.

This fund will save you time and stress. **Keep in mind it shouldn't be used for items such as holidays, clothes or home upgrades.**

If this savings goal feels overwhelming, begin to tackle it by setting aside a bigger amount to get you started, then try saving $100 a month or whatever it is that you have budgeted for and focus on having this initial goal met as soon as possible. Them bump it up from there to the next $1,000 or whatever.

By breaking the big goal down into smaller goals, you'll be able to build up your reserves in no time. I used to love seeing my savings balance go up when I went to the bank each week as part of my budget routine. So satisfying.

I know this one can seem daunting—but trust me, just get started!

No matter what you want from your finances next year or the years ahead, do what I've done all these years and put in place a plan. A plan is going to help you put your goals into action. Once you've started, don't forget to keep track of your wins and you'll be set for all that life throws at you.

I have a saying that 'nothing is impossible, only miracles take a bit longer'!

Action Steps

Before you can get started with any type of plan, you first must know what you're actually trying to accomplish. Whether it's at work, with a home project or even your finances—what does the result look like? Think about it. How hard is it to stay motivated when you're working on something if you don't even know what the point of the project is? Nobody likes to work just to work. That's why goal setting is so important. That's where you will begin your journey.

Chapter 4: The Ins and Outs

'Take one day at a time and you will eventually find your way.'

Budgeting. One of the first few topics you learn about when you study financial planning. That and debt management. Budgeting can be very simple or very complex. I'm about simplicity and so I will keep this simple, in an attempt for you to understand it better.

People usually cringe when you use the word 'budget'. Perhaps it's because some people do not understand financial literacy and that will have a lot to do with it. Or maybe they don't know where to start or are just plain lazy and it's too much of an effort for them.

Yet, I like to think about budgeting as being similar to going on a diet. It takes a lot of effort to get going at first, but by making small changes along the way, you eventually fall into an everyday healthy lifestyle. By having a budget, it will allow you to see how your actual spending compares to what you thought you were spending and will show you things you weren't aware of in your habits. Chances are, once you begin to analyse your 'outs', you may find that you're spending a lot more in some areas than you thought.

It's generally said that if the word 'budget' makes you feel anxious, then it's likely that the energy you're projecting towards money is coming from a place of lack of, rather than abundance of. The good news is that sometimes a small lifestyle tweak or mind shift is all it takes to propel yourself to prosperity.

I've been budgeting since the day I got my first job and that was many years ago. A habit that I've gotten into and still do to this day and I'm so pleased that I did it.

Usually I look at my budget at the start of each year and I'm amazed at just how much goes 'out' compared to what comes 'in'. More so now that I'm currently not working. I've saved a substantial amount to cover me for this period and so I'm doing okay. Had I not budgeted for this time of no money coming in, I think I would be feeling quite concerned and frustrated. Perhaps even distressed about the whole thing. However, I can relax and take a breather for the moment.

Okay, Where to Begin?

I started all those years ago with a piece of paper writing down where my money was going each week. Back in those days it was very simple: I paid board to my mother, petrol for my car, a certain amount went into my savings account, a bit went into an emergency account and what was left over was mine to spend. Mind you, it wasn't a lot, as I was only getting $60 a week; however, like all things at the time, it was relative. And I managed quite well.

A couple of years later and now I was married and so my budget changed quite a bit. I'm earning more money by this stage and I've also got two incomes to sort out. I added more lines and columns to my piece of paper. This gave me more room to list all our expenses that mattered the most, such as mortgage payments, car payments, insurance, groceries, etc. This is even before I considered how much to put aside for general savings and savings for those unexpected expenses

Chapter 4: The Ins and Outs

that were generally quite expensive when an event happened and we needed the cash. You could consider it as an emergency fund, or I used to call it my 'buffer' account.

It's not until you understand where your money is being spent or saved that you can truly begin to work towards a successful financial future.

Not having computers to use to put these details into a spreadsheet, I continued with a piece of paper, only it was ruled up with lines and columns, therefore, visually easier to use. It looks something like this:

Weekly	Income	Expense
Helen's wage	$650	
Husband's wage	$1000	
Total Income	**$1650**	
Mortgage payments		$400
Utilities (gas, elect)		$100
Insurance		$100
Car payments		$100
Groceries		$100
Dining out/takeaway		$45
Total Expenses		**$845**
Surplus (or – Deficit)		**$805 surplus** (or left over)

The above budget is showing that you have an $805 surplus or money left over. Remember that you still need to put some funds towards your joint savings account, your emergency reserve and some spending money for the two of you. For example, $305 for your joint savings account, $200 to the emergency fund, $100 for maybe a travel fund if you are planning on going on a holiday every year and $100 allocated for each of you.

Your personal spending money could be used for buying the occasional lunch, petrol for your car, public transport costs and I suggest having a savings account for yourself which you would put a small amount into each week. If there is any money left over from that week, you could add it to your personal savings account as an extra amount or let it mount up and use it towards something that you have seen that you liked but couldn't afford at the time.

On the other hand, the below budget is showing that you still have a surplus, although the amount left over is less than the previous one. You still need to allow for money for your joint savings account, emergency fund, that holiday account and spending money for yourself. Something has to give. This then becomes a juggling act and working with your figures and maybe going without something or being as frugal with your money as you can.

Weekly	Income	Expense
Helen's wage	$650	
Husband's wage	$1000	
Total Income	**$1650**	
Mortgage payments		$400
Utilities (gas, elect)		$100
Insurance		$100
Car payments		$100
Groceries		$200
Dining out/takeaway		$150

Chapter 4: The Ins and Outs

Total Expenses		$1050
Surplus (or – Deficit)		**$600 surplus (or left over)**

These figures are purely fictional. I am illustrating firstly what a budget looks like and secondly advising that you need to sit down and from time to time rework your planning and budget. You could end up with your expenses costing more than what your income total is and again, this is when you need to start playing with the figures.

As I have mentioned previously, doing this sort of thing is not everybody's cup of tea. I would be more than happy to have a chat with you to help you get started to put pen to paper and get you on your way.

As you can see, there are more expenses, or 'outs', if you want to remember it that way, and only two incomes, or 'ins'.

I suggest you start first with putting a spending plan together. These days there are software programs that help you to do this. If you want to keep it simple, just use a piece of paper like I did.

Your list will be made up of the following—income, which may include salary/wage or business income, interest and investment income, government benefits and any rental income.

In financial terms, your expenses are divided into two categories: fixed expenses which are expenses that are steady and ongoing, e.g. rent or mortgage payments, insurance, student loans, utilities and car payments, to name a few. Discretionary expenses, on the other hand, are those that fluctuate in cost, e.g. groceries, dining out, shopping, entertainment and lastly a trip away or holiday.

Analyse Your Spending

After setting up your spending plan, start paying attention to 'habit' areas such as coffees and daily lunches. Also look at travel, hobbies, shopping, entertainment and dining out expenses. This is where there is usually room for change.

When looking at your expenses, both fixed and discretionary, and your savings goal and you subtract them from your total income, check to see if there is a positive number left over. For example, your total income is $2,000 per week and your expenses and savings goal is $1,875. You have a positive $125 left over per week. This is what is known as a surplus, or you could say you are in the black, which is what you are aiming for. This surplus can be converted into future savings as an emergency fund, rather than touching your general savings.

If, however, you subtract your total income of $2,000 from your expenses and savings goal which is $2,200, you are left with a negative $200, and you are now 'in the red', which is what you don't want. And you are now doing what is commonly known as 'living beyond your means'. Put simply, you are spending more than you are receiving. The only way to put yourself back in the black or a positive position is to either increase your income or decrease your expenses, and to a lot of people this is easier said than done.

Chapter 4: The Ins and Outs

Controlling your spending is the same. By beginning to document and become aware of your spending habits, you'll automatically feel more comfortable and confident about your situation.

I know from my own experience and as I mentioned earlier, it does become a habit and it's a great habit to have. Keep in mind that a budget doesn't have fixed rules to live by, it's a flexible set of guidelines for you to adjust as you see fit. You can budget weekly, fortnightly, monthly or yearly. Often depending on how you are paid from your employment is how you structure your budget.

Whilst I was married, I budgeted every week. We were both paid weekly, so it made sense to have a weekly budget. Rather than one jam jar I now had several of them hidden in the back of my kitchen cupboards where I would put any money I had left over from my weekly budget amount. My weekly budget covered spending money for stockings, if I saw a dress or pair of shoes that I liked, that sort of thing. I was always amazed how quickly it would mount up. Five dollars one week, two dollars another week, which to you mightn't seem much. Let me tell you, at the time I thought it was terrific as I loved seeing the zeros in my bank book grow when I reached a certain amount and deposited it into my bank account.

Back then, I did have my own bank account apart from our joint bank account which gave me independence and set me up for life as it was a great way for me to learn about savings and having something of my own that I had to look after and grow. Sure, I had the occasional splurge and I could because I had my own money to do with as I pleased. I wasn't taking it out of our joint savings and I wasn't asking my husband at the time for money.

As I got better at doing it, I went to monthly budgeting. It also worked better that way as I was being paid monthly. It's about adjusting your budget to fit in with your life and personal goals.

Tracking your spending does take time and commitment and a conscious effort on your part, so remember to do regular checks for yourself and review your budget periodically.

Once you are in that mindset and doing a spending plan and budget on a regular basis and have conquered that, next is to think about how you are going to put something into place for setting up your savings. As I said, I had my own bank account and our joint savings account. In those days you simply went into a branch and set up a passbook account.

In this digital age, begin by paying yourself automatically by setting up a systematic transfer from your pay to your savings or an investment account and forgetting about it. This allows you to first pay yourself and treat your savings like a bill payment. But remember, whilst it's done and dusted, so to speak, don't forget to revise or check this regularly as well, particularly if your circumstances change. It doesn't have to be a big amount. Saving smaller automated increments will minimise your cash flow strain and help set the stage for a disciplined investment strategy.

Chapter 4: The Ins and Outs

Establish an Emergency Fund

In the previous chapter I mentioned about having a fund that contains a build-up of cash that will cover you for those unexpected or unplanned expenses. It's helpful to let this account grow as much as you can as it can act as a buffer for you with enough money to cover three to six months' worth of unexpected expenses. This is particularly beneficial if you're in a two-income household as it will help you out if times get tough, such as an illness, job loss or an unexpected home or car repair. This fund will save you time and stress. Keep in mind this fund shouldn't be used for items like holidays, clothes or home upgrades. It's your 'buffer' if something goes wrong and you won't need to go into your joint savings account. I first saw this on Facebook or LinkedIn. Can't remember which one; however, I reckon it's brilliant. The article is called Saving $10,000 in 52 weeks from a website called triedandTRUE Mom Jobs. It may seem a bit much to some, even aggressive to others; however, as the article states, it is doable. You just need to change your mindset as I previously mentioned in the chapter. Anything that is going to be new is going to seem difficult; however, with positive thoughts, I always say, come positive outcomes. Try your best to stick to it. Even if you change it to $5,000 in 52 weeks. That's a handy amount of money to have up your sleeve, so to speak, for those unexpected situations if you were to lose your job or an unforeseen health crisis. Better still, make this into an automated savings account and I would think that you would end up with more than $10,000 with any possible interest earned on the money. Just a thought!

Saving $10,000 in 52 weeks (table)

Week #	Deposit	Amount	Week #	Deposit	Amount
1	$125	$125	27	$175	$4,950
2	$150	$275	28	$300	$5,250
3	$175	$450	29	$125	$5,375
4	$300	$750	30	$150	$5,525
5	$125	$875	31	$175	$5,700
6	$150	$1,025	32	$300	$6,000
7	$175	$1,200	33	$125	$6,125
8	$300	$1,500	34	$150	$6,275
9	$125	$1,625	35	$175	$6,450
10	$150	$1,775	36	$300	$6,750
11	$175	$1,950	37	$125	$6,875
12	$300	$2,250	38	$150	$7,025
13	$125	$2,375	39	$175	$7,200
14	$150	$2,525	40	$300	$7,500
15	$175	$2,700	41	$125	$7,625
16	$300	$3,000	42	$150	$7,775
17	$125	$3,125	43	$175	$7,950
18	$150	$3,275	44	$300	$8,250
19	$175	$3,450	45	$125	$8,375
20	$300	$3,750	46	$150	$8,525
21	$125	$3,875	47	$175	$8,700
22	$150	$4,025	48	$300	$9,000
23	$175	$4,200	49	$200	$9,200
24	$300	$4,500	50	$225	$9,425
25	$125	$4,626	51	$250	$9,675
26	$150	$4,775	52	$325	**$10,000!**

Chapter 4: The Ins and Outs

As mentioned at the beginning of the chapter, the first two subjects I learnt about when studying for my Diploma and Advanced Diploma in Financial Planning were 1. Budgeting and 2. Debt Management.

It's important with financial literacy that you have a basic understanding of and how to implement a budget. It's also relevant that you know about what debt management is and how to manage it.

Just like we had a surplus if we had money left over in our budget which is good or we had a deficit in our budget if we had spent more than we had earned which is bad, there is good debt and bad debt and you need to understand the differences here as well.

Firstly, the simple definition of debt is **'money owed to a person or organisation you've borrowed money from, with the intent or requirement to pay the money back'.**

I'm hoping you all understand what debt is. However, you may struggle with managing it and that can be frustrating as you feel that you are getting nowhere.

Bad debts are those where you are faced with an increasing 'balance owed' on an item of decreasing value. And the perfect example here is your credit card which is used typically to pay for all sorts of things ranging from electronics, clothing, dining out and other personal objects. Some people even go so far as having more than one credit card which is such a trap.

Be Diligent With Your Debt

As you are diligent with your budget, you need to be diligent with your debt. Know your minimum repayments, balances due and interest rates of each card. Understand the effect of only paying the minimum balance each month and which balances should be paid off for those of you with more than one credit card. To me it's obvious that you would pay the credit card with the highest interest rate off first.

Remember that on top of using your credit card to buy these items, it's the bank's money that you are using to acquire these goods and services. And put simply, the bank, or any organisation for that matter, will charge you interest on the amount of money that you have spent on your credit card for these purchases. This means your purchase is costing you more than the original price that you bought it for or if you had have paid cash for it.

Unless, of course, you pay the total amount of the credit card statement for that month, rather than just paying the minimum. If you take the time to look, all the relevant details about what's owed for the month, how much in extra interest and time it is going to cost you if you only pay the minimum every month are clearly marked on the credit card statement.

For those of you with more than one credit card, my general advice would be to think about consolidating your balances to one card. Transfer your credit card balances to the one card and check first before you do this with the bank/organisation as to which card is the best to do this with, then cancel the rest and cut them up. However, be careful if you do decide to transfer your balance(s) from one card to no interest credit cards. There could be a charge of between 1% to 2% to do this. There are very few that offer a 0% balance transfer fee.

Better still, and this depends on your own personal situation, think about taking out a personal loan which generally has a smaller interest rate than credit card interest. Total the amount of your credit card debt and then borrow that amount as a personal loan. That way, you have less fees to worry about, a lower interest rate and only have to think about one payment each month. A more sensible and practical approach. As a rule, the interest rate is generally lower than that of credit card interest or other organisations offering credit facilities. A bit like rolling over multiple superannuation policies which I will speak about in Chapter 6.

For some of you, you might prefer to pay off your debt in order of smallest balance to largest, so you build momentum and get one or two of your small debts out of the way. Others may think it best to work to put extra funds towards the highest interest rate card and get that balance paid off first. Then allocate funds towards the next one and so on. Whatever you decide to do, check first with whoever it is you have your credit card(s) with.

Now for good debts, which are funds still borrowed from a bank or organisation which are used to pay for something that will either increase in value or will provide you with a benefit which can lead to increased earnings or value.

For example, good debts include things such as student loans and mortgage balances. Your mortgage gives you the ability to purchase a house, which in turn should increase over time in value.

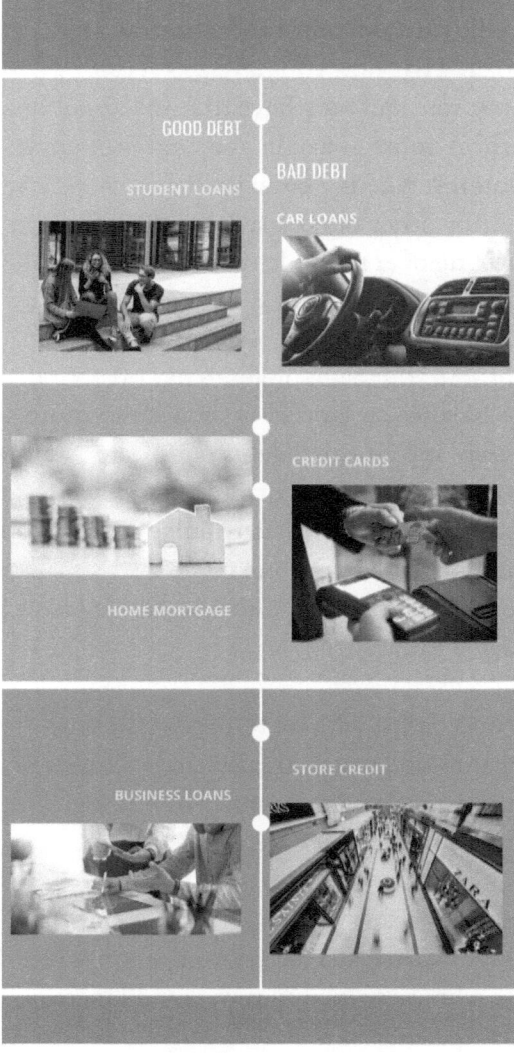

Chapter 4: The Ins and Outs

Investing in yourself, such as obtaining a student loan, helps you to obtain a higher paid job or getting a loan for leasing a vehicle helps you bring in new income for work. There are other types of good debts but I'm not going to go into those.

Debt can be a powerful tool to help you grow your wealth; however, others believe that any sort of debt is not good. Therefore, you need to decide what is best for you and for your personal circumstances.

And lastly, check first with your bank or whoever you are borrowing money from for whatever reason before you do anything that could affect your personal wealth and situation down the track.

Chapter 5: Personal Finance 101

'Take one day at a time and you will eventually find your way.'

Do You Know How Financially Fit You Are?

The subject and language of finance are often viewed as difficult and bewildering, especially to those of you who are not schooled in the art of accountancy. They need not be.

Why It Is Important to Understand Basic Finance

I believe that we should have at least a basic understanding of the subject and language of finance, particularly if we want to have a stress-free life that's been planned and thought about on a regular basis with regards to our financial well-being. Most of us take the time to look after ourselves which is very important as I have a saying that 'if you don't have your health you don't have your wealth'.

If we are unable to work because of some illness or whatever reason, then with no income, you will most likely struggle and creating wealth or even maintaining a solid financial foundation will be hard. To me, health and wealth go hand in hand.

Without a grasp of some basic financial concepts, it can be easy to take what appears to be a wise decision, but one that nevertheless is ill informed and one that adversely affects the financial health aspects of our life. Those not comfortable with finance and the appropriate use of its language invariably find themselves struggling to cope as effectively as they could. In contrast, those that do are able to focus on what is important and generally succeed in making and taking better informed decisions.

Whilst finance is not rocket science, it is nevertheless a challenge for many people, especially those who perceive themselves not to be good at maths. However, as with any life skill, finance can be learnt. All it takes is a willingness to try and to take the time to learn more about it. There is just so much knowledge that is available to everyone these days that there is really no excuse.

I briefly discussed and tried to explain about debt in a previous chapter. This chapter is not so much about understanding debt, but debt consolidation and what it means and why to consider it as an option for you if your situation would warrant it.

Debt Consolidation

What is it, you ask? It's a process whereby you take out a loan that pays off two or more other loans that you may have, for example, a car loan, and perhaps you took out a loan for an overseas holiday. Consider taking out a debt consolidation loan and rolling over your short-term debt you have into your home mortgage loan, either at the time of purchase or later when you are considering buying a home.

By doing this, borrowers consolidate what loans they have into one in order to reduce their finance costs. Usually, the interest rate on the mortgage is below that of the short-term debt they have. Borrowers also like the convenience of making fewer payments.

However, be careful and make sure you seek proper advice before doing this as consolidation that reduces the borrower's total monthly payments while eliminating their short-term debt may encourage them to build up that debt all over again. This could result in so much debt they never get out from under it and this we don't want. To consolidate intelligently, borrowers need to compare and consider all their options.

Life After Consolidation

Borrowers who consolidate should use any monthly savings to accelerate the pay down of principal on their mortgage(s). Even better is to shorten the term on the new mortgage(s) so that the new payment is close to the old payment.

However, some borrowers interpret debt consolidation as a licence to take on more non-mortgage debt. A few years later, they look to consolidate again. If their house has appreciated enough, they may be able to, but sooner or later they run out of equity. They trapped themselves. Don't let it happen to you. Seek professional advice if this is something you are considering and assess your financial situation.

Steps to Debt Success

It could be your mortgage, your credit card or a personal loan. Whatever your debts are, as they accumulate it can feel like they are difficult to manage. But don't lose confidence. While there's no overnight 'quick fix' for debt problems, there are steps you can take to go from debt stress to debt success.

Create a Debt 'Hit List'

Start by listing all your debts, including the fees and the interest rate which applies to each one. This will help give you a holistic view of your debts. Chances are the interest rate on your credit card will be at the higher end of the scale, but it can vary depending on the type of purchase you made on the card.

Analyse Your Spending and Create a Budget

A detailed look at what's going out over a set period could help you identify your current spending habits and distinguish between essential and non-essential spending. Consider whether you can redirect any non-essential expenses to make extra debt repayments and then draw up a household budget to make it easier for you to stick to your plan.

Pay Off Highest Interest Rate Debts First

Once you have identified how much cash you can put towards making extra repayments, work out which debt to eliminate first. Due to the power of compound interest, it could make sense to allocate additional repayments to the debt with the highest interest rate. In the meantime, keep making the minimum repayments on all your remaining debts.

Once you've paid off one of your debts, put the money you've been using to pay off this debt towards extra payments on debt number two on your hit list and so on.

If you have equity in your home and several small-term debts you want to clear quickly, you may be able to refinance your home loan and use the equity to pay off the short-term debt. Make sure you speak to your broker or financial adviser for advice specific to your situation.

Don't Be Frightened to Ask for Help If You Need It

As I always say, 'if you don't ask, you don't get'. It's very important. If you are in serious debt and struggling to meet your regular minimum repayments, speak honestly to your lender about your situation. By making them aware that you may be having problems paying back your debt, by speaking up, it could help you take back control of your finances rather than your financial circumstances spiralling out of control.

Accounts Payable and Accounts Receivable

I also want to explain in simple language—what is accounts payable and accounts receivable? It came to my attention when I did a presentation to a group of first-year tertiary students in February 2020 on project management. The students had been broken up into groups and were given a subject that they had to work on with regards to project management.

As I mingled amongst the students after my presentation, I asked each group what their designated subject was. 'Accounts payable and accounts receivable,' one group muttered to me. I asked them did they know what accounts payable and accounts receivable was. To my astonishment not one of them had any idea what accounts payable and accounts receivable was. They couldn't even begin to tell me in basic terms what it was.

This got me thinking that perhaps there are other people who lack the knowledge and understanding of what accounts payable and accounts receivable is and how it works, etc.

Simply put, accounts payable (AP) is a term that refers to money that a person or business must pay to someone or another business within a certain period of time when they have purchased something, be it a product or service. It is the unpaid invoices, bills or statements for goods and services provided by outside contractors, traders or suppliers. These bills or invoices must be paid according to the company's terms and conditions which can vary from supplier to supplier.

The purpose of accounts payable is to provide checks and balances for all outgoing payments to vendors/suppliers for their goods or services. The aim of this process is to make certain that only bills which are legitimate are paid and enough security is built into the process.

The role of accounts payable involves providing financial, administrative and clerical support to the organisation. The person appointed to the role is to complete payments and control expenses by receiving payments, plus processing, verifying and reconciling invoices. A typical accounts payable job description also highlights the day-to-day management of all payment cycle activities in a timely and efficient manner. These are also regarded as a liability on a balance sheet.

Accounts Payable Duties and Responsibilities of the Job

As a vital team member of the finance team, it's important that an accounts payable job description includes:

- Keeping track of all payments and expenditures, including payroll, purchase orders, invoices, statements, etc.
- Reconciling processed work by verifying entries and comparing system reports to balances
- Maintaining historical records
- Paying employees by verifying expense reports and preparing pay cheques
- Paying vendors by scheduling pay cheques and ensuring payment is received for outstanding credit; generally responding to all vendor enquiries regarding finance
- Preparing analyses of accounts and producing monthly reports
- Continuing to improve the payment process.

Whereas on the other hand, accounts receivable is the opposite. Accounts payable is money going out of a company and accounts receivable is money coming into a company. It's about collecting money back into the company's coffers, instead of accounts payable as money going out of the company's bank accounts, to put it more simply.

Or on broader terms, accounts receivable are debts owed to a company by its customers for goods or services that have been delivered or used but not yet paid for.

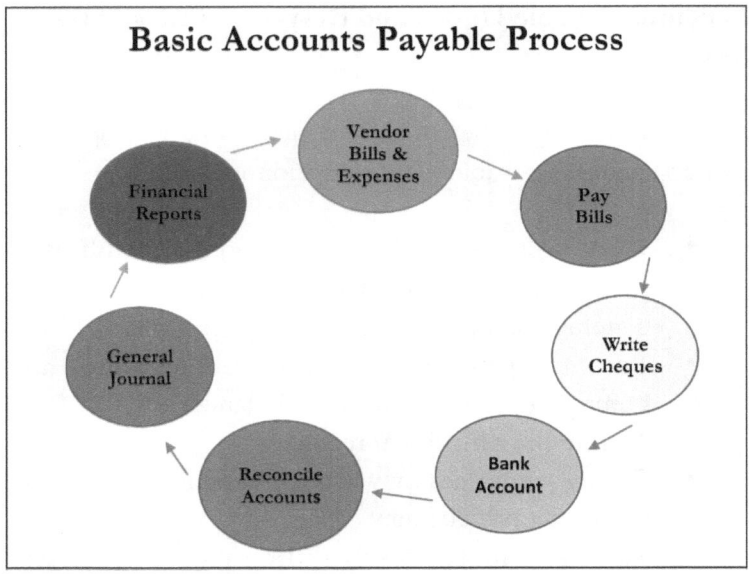

These are generally in the form of invoices raised by a business and delivered to the customer for payment within an agreed time frame. Accounts receivable is shown in a balance sheet as an asset. It is one of a series of accounting transactions dealing with the billing of a customer for goods and services that the customer has ordered.

Both accounts payable and accounts receivable are financial records of an organisation. To check the overall balance of credits and debits is the major part of every company's financial growth.

Accounts receivable is an asset. To be more specific, it is considered a current asset because it is money that is expected to be received within one year. In contrast, an account payable is a current liability.

Chapter 5: Personal Finance 101

I hope what I have written helps to explain two financial terms in more basic language for you. It's not all that relevant to your own financial well-being; however, if you understand that one is money going out of your purse and the other is money coming back into your purse, then it might help you to understand it better.

Credit Cards

We all know about credit cards, don't we—or do we? What we do know about credit cards is that just about every one of us has one, whether it's in its original plastic form or an app on our phone or watch.

We know that credit cards charge interest on things we buy and are primarily used for short-term funding of our purchases. There are just so many credit cards available out there that really, it's quite scary, particularly if used wrongly or without proper advice and knowledge.

The credit card you choose will generally depend on what you want to use your credit card for and the perks you may receive whenever you do if you choose a credit card that offers such.

Range of Credit Cards

Low rate credit cards are as the name implies, those that come with a lower average interest rate. Interest rates are kept low on this type of card because they don't offer perks like reward programs or high credit limits. If you are considering the no-frills approach that's generally easier to manage, then look at a low rate credit card, for example.

However, keep an eye out for what rate the 'low' label applies. A low rate credit card may have a low purchase rate, but a higher-than-average cash advance rate. Make sure you check all the facts before entering into an agreement for a credit card. I would also be very mindful of taking out a cash advance by using your credit card. This is something I suggest you don't do, unless of course you are absolutely desperate to get some cash.

Platinum credit cards. Unlike low rate credit cards, platinum cards are geared towards those searching for high credit limits and extensive rewards programs. As it suggests, these cards do come with higher interest rates and annual fees. However, the idea is that those taking out a platinum credit card can afford these costs as they're marketed towards those with higher incomes.

Balance transfer cards. If you have existing credit card debt, balance transfer cards can be a helpful debt management tool. They charge no interest on a balance you transfer from your old credit card for a limited time. This means you can concentrate on clearing your debt without being charged more interest on top of it.

Just remember that you'll still be charged interest on new purchases, often straight away, without the benefit of interest-free days. If you do decide to get a balance transfer card, get the customer adviser in the bank or wherever you are getting your new card from to cut up your old cards in front of you. Wow, this will be quite liberating and means you can now focus on paying off your debt.

Rewards credit cards. Ones that are attached to a reward program. The dollars you spend will earn you reward points. Credit card providers will allow you to exchange these points through the relevant reward program for things like gift cards, home goods and electronics.

If you plan on using your credit card regularly, they can be a competitive choice. Consider how you plan to use your card and how closely this matches with the card's reward program. For example, if you regularly use your credit card at a local supermarket, you may want to consider a credit card that lets you earn points that can be redeemed at these shops.

Frequent flyer cards. One of the most popular types of reward credit cards are those that offer frequent flyer points with airlines. These cards are like rewards points; however, you earn frequent flyer points instead based on the amount you spend when flying or doing shopping online within their website. They can be spent on flights or upgrade with major airlines. If you make regular plane trips for work or to visit family, or if you love to travel, this card type may suit you.

What to Look for in a Credit Card

Here are a few things to consider when shopping around for a credit card:

- **Credit card purpose:** How do you plan on using your credit card? For everyday shopping or major purchases only? For buying overseas or when you travel? To transfer an existing balance? Narrow down your purpose so you can compare apples with apples.

- **Interest rates:** Credit cards can charge different rates for purchases, cash advances and balance transfers. Also, keep an eye out for introductory, promotional, or 'honeymoon' rates that revert to a higher one after a certain period. Knowing what rates you may be charged before applying can keep you from growing debt.
- **Interest-free periods:** How long you'll have to pay back your purchases before you're charged credit card interest. The higher number of days, the more breathing room to make repayments.
- **Reward programs and extras:** Reward programs let you earn points on your everyday spending that can be exchanged for goods or transferred into frequent flyer points. Some credit cards also offer extras such as travel insurance. These programs and extras typically incur higher annual fees.
- **Fees and charges:** Are there any extra costs, such as annual fees, or charges for overseas purchases? Consider whether the credit card's benefits would likely be worth these costs.

Can Anyone Get a Credit Card?

No, not everyone will be approved for every credit card. However, it is easier to be approved for a credit card than some other forms of finance, like a home loan, as you don't need to offer up a deposit to be approved.

But you will need to meet credit card eligibility criteria, such as:

Chapter 5: Personal Finance 101

- Being an Australian citizen or permanent resident
- 18 years old or over
- No history of bankruptcy
- Meet minimum income requirements (can range from $10,000 to $1,000,000 and higher for platinum and above cards)
- Good credit rating. Credit card providers will assess your eligibility at different scales, depending on the type of card you're applying for. For example, if you're applying for a platinum credit card and you don't meet the minimum income required, your application is more likely to be rejected.

When applying for a credit card, you'll need to provide the following:

- Proof of income: salaries or wages
- Proof of employment: two or more recent payslips
- Photo ID (driver's licence, proof of age card or passport)
- Additional assets and income (such as a savings account or managed investments)
- Credit history
- Tax file number
- Details of any existing loans, such as personal loans, a lease or other credit cards
- Recent tax returns, particularly if you're self-employed.

How Much Do I Have to Pay on My Credit Card?

All credit cards have minimum repayment requirements. These are usually a percentage of your total balance (2 – 3.5%); however, they can be a dollar figure—usually around $20. It's highly encouraged that you make more than the minimum repayment requirements, however, or it can take you years to pay off an outstanding balance.

For example, Mark has an outstanding credit card balance of $10,000 at an interest rate of 18%. His card has a minimum repayment amount of $20 or 2% (whichever is higher). If he only made minimum repayments to this debt, it would take him 43 years and 11 months to pay off his balance. However, if he made higher monthly repayments of $400, it would only take two years and seven months to pay off his balance.

How Do You Compare Credit Cards?

Now you know the type of card you want and the extras to keep an eye out for, it's time to narrow down your options. The best way to compare credit cards is to do your research and use comparison tables and let me tell you, there are heaps of websites that have comparison tables and information for you to help when considering taking out a credit card.

Comparison tables are a helpful way to compare things equally, side by side. You can view a range of credit card options in a table that outlines some of the more significant costs and features. These include the purchase rate, annual fees, maximum interest free days and late payment fees. Filter down your options to create a shortlist of credit cards.

Make up a shortlist of those you think are appropriate for your needs and then it's worth checking out the Key Facts Sheet for each card you may be considering. These are kept on the credit card providers' website. They offer more detail

Chapter 5: Personal Finance 101

on the cards you're interested in, such as a breakdown of all fees and interest rates.

What's more, your credit card could have features to help you to stay on top of your spending in the future. Some credit cards have a feature whereby you receive notifications when you're close to your card limit or a limit that you specify. This is super handy when life gets a bit frantic.

Credit card debt is one of the most common causes of debt stress, but there's no reason to lose confidence. Take the time to explore your credit card options as you may find one that suits your lifestyle better than the one you have now.

And this again all leads back to budgeting, spending and planning your financial situation on a regular basis and seeking financial advice if you are considering any of these options. Each situation is different.

Chapter 6: Superannuation—A Basic Introduction to Understanding Super

Did you know that 'about 90% of women will retire with inadequate savings to fund a comfortable lifestyle in retirement'? (The Association of Superannuation Funds of Australia, ASFA 2015).

Whether you're just starting out in your career, or getting close to retirement age, superannuation is very important.

It's something that most people do not think about until they hit their '50s and it's generally at this point they start thinking of their retirement plan.

For those of us born from 1946 –1964 (Baby Boomers), generally speaking, women will be in a situation where their superannuation balance will be low as superannuation only came in in the '90s. Whereas those born after the '90s should have a more substantial superannuation offering when they reach retirement age.

Superannuation is your money and by making regular and smart superannuation contributions over the course of your working life, you are more likely to eventually have significant savings that can help pay for your life after work.

Here are several reasons why superannuation is incredibly important:

Retirement can last a long time

Once you have retired (or semi-retired), your main source of income will cease or diminish. For this reason, it's very important that you have enough funds to cover you for the rest of your life. Lots of Australians underestimate how much money they will need for their retirement. Keep in mind also that people are generally living longer.

The Age Pension may not be enough

While the Australian Government offers an Age Pension to eligible individuals, the amount you receive may not be enough to give you the lifestyle or fulfil the financial obligations you currently have. After working hard for so many years, it's important to enjoy your retirement. You may, for instance, have great travel plans for when you retire. Or you may wish to take up some new hobbies, sign up for some new classes or take up some new memberships since you're no longer working. If this is the case, it can be beneficial to supplement any Age Pension by drawing on your superannuation, for example as additional income.

It's an effective way to save over the long term

The Australian Government has provided tax concessions to superannuation which helps to make it one of the **best long-term investments**. Your superannuation is essentially money put aside for your retirement—your savings. Superannuation is a long-term investment, so every dollar you save could make a significant difference when you retire.

Chapter 6: Superannuation

One of the main features of super is that you typically can't access your money until you retire after reaching your 'preservation age'. The preservation age is 55 years until 30 June 2015, after which it will gradually increase to age 60. The table below outlines the preservation age applying to an individual:

Persons born:	Preservation Age
After 30 June 1964	60
1 July 1963 – 30 June 1964 (inclusive)	59
1 July 1962 – 30 June 1963 (inclusive)	58
1 July 1961 – 30 June 1962 (inclusive)	57
1 July 1960 – 30 June 1961 (inclusive)	56
Before 1 July 1960	55

So even if retirement seems a long way off, it's important to get your superannuation account started as soon as you enter the workforce—and regularly review your super to ensure that you are on track to achieving sufficient funds for your retirement.

Making the most of superannuation every way you can and as early as possible is even more critical for women. Statistically, women's salaries are generally lower than males and many women will take time out of the workforce to raise a family and some may return in a part-time capacity, or not at all.

Women generally retire earlier than men do and have a longer life expectancy—89 years for women and 86 for men.

So, for women, the need to take control of their superannuation is paramount and the time to act is now!

For the most part, people do not understand super and how it works, and rightly so. It seems with each respective new government comes new rules and changes to super that unless you are a financial planner or accountant, you will struggle to understand what it all means and how it is going to affect you down the track. In this chapter, I will share with you my strategies on how investing in superannuation can lead to a more comfortable retirement.

Super is a great tax-effective vehicle to build wealth and it often makes sense to invest as much as you can as early as you can while you are still working. Most Australians fund their retirement from their superannuation.

How Much Superannuation Will Be Enough?

Generally, Australian employers are required to contribute at least 9.5% of your wage/salary to your super so long as you are 18 years old or over and you earn $450 or more before tax in a month. However, will this be enough for you to live comfortably in retirement? The amount of superannuation you may need depends on your personal circumstances, such as your age at retirement, desired retirement income and estate planning wishes.

Chapter 6: Superannuation

> **Speaking of estate planning, did you know that if you haven't made a will, it's up to the discretion of the trustee of the super fund to determine who should receive your super death benefit when you die. It just doesn't go to your spouse and/or children as many people assume it does!**

To determine if you are on track to reach your retirement savings goal, you will also need to consider the following:

- How much time you have to accumulate your superannuation, especially if you plan to take time out of the workforce
- The cost of living and effects of inflation in the future
- The increase in life expectancies, meaning a longer retirement period
- Your attitude to risk and return
- How much you have already saved for your retirement
- If you have dependents to consider
- The type of lifestyle you wish to live in retirement, and lastly
- Any other investments you may have.

The earlier you put a considered super strategy in place, the more chance you have of achieving your target at retirement.

Some super-boosting strategies you may not be aware of and the one that I recommend everyone considers is to look at salary sacrificing, which is a topic that I will go into more detail in the next chapter.

Consolidating Your Superannuation (Rolling Over Multiple Policies)

You may well ask, what does this mean? To put it simply, and I know from my own experience, it's where we have held a number of jobs over the years and this is especially relevant to those of you who have taken temp assignments or done contract work and you may have accumulated multiple superannuation accounts. Most likely you will be paying fees on each of these policies and you could be paying for multiple insurance coverage which could be costing you money and reducing your super balances. Therefore, it's wise to consider consolidating all your super accounts into one policy by what's known as 'rolling them over'.

There are numerous sites that can help you track down any lost super accounts you may have that you have forgotten about. For example, click on the link www.yourlostsuper.com.au and it will take you to a page where you enter your details and they will come back to you and let you know whether you have any super account balances owing that you are unaware of.

Did you know that there is $18 billion dollars of lost or unclaimed superannuation out there in the abyss that could be yours? Try it out, you could get a surprise!

Consolidating your superannuation into one policy can result in your money working harder to increase your retirement savings. You can also keep better track of just one policy rather than numerous ones and it also means you will only be paying one set of fees.

> **Remember, before rolling over your policies from each fund to one fund, check and be comfortable with any applicable exit or withdrawal fees. Also check if any benefits, such as insurance, will be lost if you leave that fund. Your main super fund should be able to instruct you on how to complete the necessary transfer forms.**
>
> **For those of you who don't know where to start, I'd be more than happy to assist you in organising this and getting it done for you for a small fee.**

Choosing the Fund That Is Right for You

Most Australians have a choice when it comes to superannuation in selecting the super fund that they want their money to go into. It's worth thinking about your needs and checking out the options that each fund might give you, instead of blindly leaving it with your employer's default superannuation fund.

Again, from my own experience, I wished I had checked out the super fund that one of my employers was putting my contributions into. It wasn't until down the track I found out that I was paying higher fees than some other super funds and paying expensive premiums for insurance. Had I done my homework more diligently, I most likely would have come out with a bigger super balance than I had at the time.

More then would have meant more now.

The other option to consider when selecting a super fund is to consider your attitude to risk. By this I mean whether you have your contributions in a conservative, balanced, high growth or cash portfolio. Each one of these categories has certain levels of risk attached to them and you need to be mindful of what each one represents.

It's also good to investigate what your current superannuation funds are invested in, i.e. shares, international or Australian companies, property, fixed interest and cash. You will also need to consider the fund's investment performance, investment choices, insurance coverage and fees—these elements will all affect the ultimate balance of your super.

If you are considering switching funds, you should also evaluate all of the above for the new fund as well—especially the availability and your eligibility for the type and level of insurance cover you require.

Most people don't understand this side of superannuation, so feel free to contact me and I'm happy to have a look at your policy and try to explain it to you in a more user-friendly way.

Failing having a chat with me, you may wish to seek help from a financial adviser to ensure you make a decision that is right for you.

Lastly, and this is a fact that a lot of people are not aware of within superannuation:

Who Gets Your Super When You Die? A Guide to Death Benefit Nominations

If you have a valid will in place when you die, most of us assume it's simply a matter of our executors taking care of all the paperwork and paying out our remaining assets to our beneficiaries in the proportions listed in the will.

But in fact, when it comes to your super account, what you state in your will doesn't necessarily decide who gets your retirement savings, as the trustee of your super fund is not required to take your wishes into account.

So if you are wanting to leave your super to your spouse/ partner, or whoever, you must complete what is called a 'binding nomination' form through your superannuation fund.

What Is a Binding Death Benefit Nomination?

Superannuation is not an estate asset; on death it does not automatically flow to the estate of the deceased.

Put simply, a binding death benefit nomination is a legally binding nomination that allows you to advise the trustee who is to receive your superannuation benefit in the event of your death. For a nomination to be binding, it must be 'valid'. One of the requirements of validity is that only 'dependents' can be nominated. Depending on your circumstances, however, you can nominate one dependent or several dependents. For the purposes of superannuation law, a dependent includes:

- a spouse (including de facto, opposite and same sex)
- children of any age (including adopted or ex-nuptial)
- any person(s) financially dependent on the member
- any person(s) in an interdependency relationship with the member (applicable since 1 July 2004)
- a legal personal representative (LPR).

Providing Certainty

One of the biggest benefits you receive from having a binding death benefit nomination in place is peace of mind. This is especially the case if you have multiple beneficiaries (e.g. from previous marriages) who may have a claim on your death benefit.

In this case, you can nominate with reasonable certainty who you wish to receive your death benefit or, if being paid to more than one beneficiary, who receives what proportion.

Ease and speed

Another advantage of a binding death benefit nomination is the ease and speed with which a death benefit can be paid. If your beneficiary needs quick access to your benefit, a binding death benefit nomination may allow a timelier distribution of your assets and your beneficiary won't have to wait for the trustee or the deceased estate to determine the distribution.

How to Make a Valid Binding Death Benefit Nomination

To make a valid nomination you must follow the procedures explained below. The nomination must:

- be made to the trustee in writing and clearly set out the proportion of the benefit to be paid to each person nominated. It may also include the type of benefit payment (such as a lump sum and/or an income stream)

Chapter 6: Superannuation

- be signed by the member in the presence of two witnesses over 18 years of age and who are not nominated as beneficiaries
- contain a signed witness declaration
- be sent to the trustee (a nomination will not be valid until it's received by the trustee).

Once you have made the nomination, it will be valid for three years from the date it was signed. You can renew, change, update or revoke a nomination at any time.

If the nomination is valid, the trustee must follow it, even if your circumstances have changed. For example, if you nominate your spouse and you separate, but have not yet obtained a divorce, the nomination remains valid and binds the trustee unless the nomination has been amended, revoked or has expired.

Now you might find this chapter overwhelming and rightly so as superannuation is such a confusing and complex beast. But it needn't be. However, it is something that is here to stay, most likely ever changing. Nonetheless, it's an ideal tool for saving towards one's retirement and could mean the difference between enjoying a comfortable lifestyle or relying entirely on the Age Pension, which if you are renting is not a good option.

And I say this because the stats are telling us that:

1. Older people make up a considerable proportion of Australia's population—in 2017, over one in seven people were aged 65 and over.

2. One in six (16%) of all homeless people on Census night were aged 55 or over—that's around 18,600 people.

3. Homelessness is a growing problem for older Australians and will likely continue to increase over time due to an ageing population and declining rates of home ownership among older people. Over the last decade, the number of older homeless people increased by 49%, with the largest changes measured in people aged 65 – 74 and 55 – 64. Although older women do not account for most homeless people, they represent a rapidly growing demographic in the homeless population—increasing by 31% from 2011. Factors such as domestic violence, relationship breakdown, financial difficulty and limited superannuation can put older women at risk of homelessness.

Women and Super

Did you know that more than 80% of women are currently retiring with insufficient superannuation savings to fund a comfortable lifestyle? In fact, the average super account balance for women when they retire is around $115,000 less than the average for men. And the reasons are obvious, as I have mentioned above—taking time out to raise a family, part-time or low-paid employment.

No matter what the reason, there is no doubt women have a much bigger task when it comes to saving for their retirement. That's why it's important all women take simple steps to help boost their super savings.

Chapter 6: Superannuation

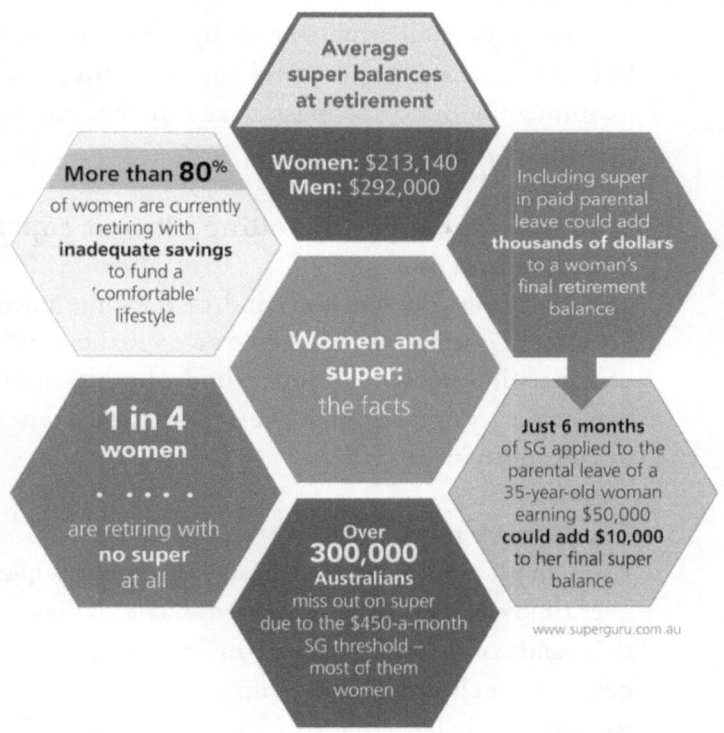

Therefore, looking regularly at your super and making sure that it is doing the right thing for you is going to be very important for women in particular as we head into retirement.

Super Sorter Power Hour

Taking 60 minutes today to sort your super could add thousands to your retirement savings. So here is what you should consider doing:

1. **Check your super savings**
   Get to know your super better by checking your balance regularly, as well as the insurance and investment options; you must make sure they are the best fit for your circumstances.

2. **Simplify your super by rolling all your super accounts into one**
   Consolidating your accounts and/or tracking down your lost or unclaimed super could save you thousands of dollars in unnecessary super fund administration fees, which over time can make a massive difference to your retirement savings.

3. **Plan to save more**
   Even small additional contributions to your super over time can help boost your retirement savings by thousands of dollars. These extra contributions can help you catch up on the savings time you missed, for example, when you took time out to have a baby.

Now if you find that you are still struggling with understanding superannuation and what's best for you, I'm here to help you!

Chapter 7: Building Your Nest Egg

'I believe that through knowledge and discipline, financial peace is possible for all of us'—Dave Ramsey.

Following on from the previous chapter on superannuation, I mentioned that superannuation is your money and by making regular and smart contributions to your super, you are more likely to eventually have significant savings that can help pay for your life after work.

A smart way to contribute to your super is to 'salary sacrifice'. This is not to be confused with salary packaging which I will touch on further in this chapter.

To 'salary sacrifice' is to contribute a portion of your pre-tax income into your super account. It's a powerful way to grow your super balance—especially in your younger years when you have time on your side for those contributions to grow and boost your super balance.

One other benefit of salary sacrificing is that it will most likely reduce the income tax you pay. Therefore, you will receive a slightly higher take-home pay amount as a result of these personal pre-tax deductions. This occurs as your contributions are taxed by your super fund at 15%, the same as your employer's contributions. For most people this will be lower than their marginal tax rate. This method of contributing to your super is beneficial to those of you who are earning $37,000 and above. Therefore, it is considered as a tax effective strategy. In superannuation terms, these pre-tax contributions are what's known as concessional contributions.

For you to salary sacrifice, you will need to check with your employer first to make sure you are able to contribute to your super account in this way, as it is the employer who does this for you via your super fund.

The total amount that may be contributed to your superannuation is capped at $25,000 per annum. Just make sure that if you decide to contribute to a salary sacrificing arrangement with your employer, you do not exceed this capped amount.

Salary sacrificing by way of including personal pre-tax deductions into your super account is an important strategy to consider regardless of whether you plan on having a family or taking a career break.

Put simply, the pros to salary sacrifice to super are:

1. You will pay less tax.
2. You will boost your retirement savings.
3. These additional contributions are concessionally taxed, i.e. at 15%.

However, you need to be mindful of the cons:

1. Your money will be locked away until you reach preservation age (see table in chapter on Superannuation to refresh your memory of your preservation age).
2. There are limits on how much you can salary sacrifice into super. Your employer should be able to assist you with how much extra you can put into your super via salary sacrificing.

3. You will also need to meet a condition of release. The five most common conditions of release are:
    - Being over preservation age and retiring
    - Being over preservation age and starting a transition-to-retirement income stream (TRIS)
    - Being 60 or over and ceasing an employment arrangement
    - Being 65 or over
    - Death.

There are additional conditions of release that will allow you to access your super early if you meet strict eligibility criteria as outlined below:

- On compassionate grounds
- If you're suffering severe financial hardship
- If you're diagnosed with a terminal medical condition
- If you're temporarily incapacitated
- If you're permanently incapacitated.

Make Sure Your Employer Contributions Don't Drop

Before you salary sacrifice, make sure your employer will continue to calculate your Super Guarantee payments on your gross income, before the salary sacrifice amount is deducted. It's best to get this agreement in writing.

Check Your Super Is Being Paid to You

Make sure you're getting what you're entitled to. Your employer must transfer super to your super fund at least once a quarter, although some choose to do it more often. Check you are receiving the right amount of super. You can do this by logging into your online super account or contacting your super fund.

If you think you're not getting paid the correct amount of super, talk to your employer. Ask how often they're paying your super, which fund they're paying it into and how much they're paying.

If your employer is not paying your super, report it to the ATO.

Besides utilising pre-tax contributions to add to your super balance, it is also possible to make contributions to your super on an after-tax basis. These are known as non-concessional contributions. They simply add to your super balance and it grows from there.

For most people, the limit (as from 2017 – 2018) on this type of contribution is currently $100,000 per annum or $300,000 over a three-year period. However, restrictions may apply if you have made previous similar contributions or you have a significant balance already in super (over $1.6m).

As with all super contributions, you need to be mindful that your super is generally not accessible until you reach preservation age, or you meet one of the conditions of release. Therefore, you need to carefully consider whether these funds might be needed for something else prior to retirement.

Both pre-tax and post-tax contribution limit rules can be tricky and particularly if you're planning to maximise your contributions. You should certainly seek advice before committing to a contribution strategy.

Chapter 7: Building Your Nest Egg

The Government Superannuation Co-Contribution Scheme

There are other ways to increase your super contributions besides pre-tax and post-tax contributions. For those of you who are not on a high income, you can grow your super faster by getting a little boost from the government.

Under the scheme, those earning a total income up to $38,564 (for 2019 – 20 indexed each year) or less and you make a voluntary after-tax or post-tax contribution to your super account by 30 June each year, the ATO will confirm your eligibility to receive the government co-contribution up to a maximum of $500 per year.

The government co-contribution amount reduces if you earn more than $38,564 and cuts off for those earning a total income of $53,564 or more. This is a great incentive for you to put a little extra money towards your superannuation.

An example of how much you could get is shown below:

Your total income*	Your voluntary after-tax contribution	Maximum co-contribution
Up to $38,564	$1,000	$500
$53,564	Any amount	$0

The co-contribution gets paid directly into your account after you've lodged your tax return for that year, if your super fund has your TFN (Tax File Number).

As mentioned previously, you need to be eligible to receive the government co-contribution. Therefore, it's important to know that you are eligible if:

- you make voluntary after-tax contributions to a super fund during the financial year
- your total income is less than $53,564 p.a.
- you're under 71 years old at the end of the financial year
- you lodge an income tax return for the relevant financial year
- you have not held a temporary resident visa at any time during the financial year
- you earned 10% or more of your total income from running a business, or from eligible employment or a combination of both
- your non-concessional (after-tax) contributions did not exceed the cap for that financial year
- your total superannuation balance, at 30 June of the previous financial year, is less than $1.6M.

Super Spouse Contributions

For those of you who are married (including same-sex partners) or in a de facto relationship, you might want to consider spouse contributions to your super. A spouse can make post-tax contributions into their partner's super fund. They may be eligible for a tax offset of 18% on up to the first $3,000 of spouse contributions; a maximum tax offset of $540 if the partner is low- or no-income earner.

Contributing to super via spouse contributions can be an effective way to grow your retirement savings, while reducing your tax.

Chapter 7: Building Your Nest Egg

> **Case study for spouse contributions**
>
>
> John and Lisa are in a de facto relationship. John, 30, works as a teacher and earns $75,000 annually. Lisa, 28, works casually and earns $37,000 a year.
>
> John has decided to contribute $120 a fortnight into Lisa's super account ($3,120 a year). Because Lisa is a low-income earner, the first $3,000 of John's contribution qualifies for the maximum tax offset of 18%. John receives the full tax offset, reducing the tax payable on his income by $540.

Above is a case study which may help you to understand spouse contributions to your super.

This strategy is particularly relevant for women who plan to take time out from working to have a family, for example. You can still build a super nest egg with the help of your spouse's contributions into your super account.

Contributions Splitting

And lastly, this strategy is useful when one partner is older than the other, of preservation age and therefore able to access their super. Or in retirement as a couple and both parties are looking to get the most out of their retirement from their super. Making contributions to your spouse's super account is a great way to help if they have a low superannuation balance—either due to time out of the workforce or earning a low wage/salary.

This is what's known as contributions splitting. This is where couples split their super contributions, i.e. they can transfer certain contributions from one spouse's super account to the other's account.

When you split super contributions, you apply to your super fund to transfer to your spouse a portion of the before-tax (concessional) contributions made to your super account during the financial year.

What Are the Benefits of Doing This?

Super splitting can be an effective way of providing superannuation to a non-working or low-income spouse. In addition to growing their balance, the contributions could also pay for the cost of their insurance cover if they are taking a break from the workforce.

Contribution splitting to a spouse could be used as a long-term strategy to even out the super balances between partners and keep individual balances below the limits set by the Australian Government. This could help maximise the combined total of super savings that can be transferred to a tax-free environment when you retire.

For example:

- Splitting contributions to keep individual balances below $500,000 means each partner can take advantage of the carry forward rules on their before-tax contributions for up to five years—maximising the amount you can add to your super savings for a tax-effective retirement.

- For members with superannuation balances that may exceed the transfer balance cap ($1.6 million), super splitting can keep both balances under the cap, maximising the amount you can hold tax-free in retirement.

Case study—splitting for a balance boost

Larry has a superannuation balance of $400,000. Last financial year his employer made $15,000 in Superannuation Guarantee (SG) contributions to his super account. After speaking to a financial adviser, Larry decides to apply to his super fund to split the maximum amount of his before-tax contributions to his wife Monica, who has taken time off work to care for their three children.

Larry can split 85% of his contributions, adding $12,750 to Monica's retirement savings.

Not all superannuation funds allow super splitting and there are rules and an eligibility criteria that you need to be aware of and what you can and can't split.

Before you do anything with regards to any of the strategies I have shown above, make sure you get professional advice.

I've included the above information to make you aware of what's available to you to help you grow your retirement fund.

As mentioned earlier in the chapter, there is also what is known as salary packaging which I believe is different to what I'm trying to explain about with salary sacrificing.

This involves an arrangement between you and your employer where you pay for some items or services straight from your pre-tax salary. You can salary package computers, cars, childcare and school fees, for example. However, this is up to the discretion of your employer and is generally something that is negotiated between both parties as to whether it's going to be beneficial to you. With salary packaging these kinds of items/services, you will generally be up for FPT (Fringe Benefits Tax) and I have never been one for salary packaging in this instance.

Personally, because I had my own secretarial business and was self-employed many years, I made use of non-concessional contributions to my personal super fund. Then some years back I learnt about the benefits of salary sacrificing in the true sense of the word and I wish now that I had 'salary sacrificed' much sooner than I did. I'm positive my retirement balance would be far greater than it is now. Although it is certainly better than nothing at all.

I also took advantage of the government co-contribution scheme when I was self-employed and wasn't earning a huge wage. So, I know that that scheme does work and it did help to get those extra dollars when it was most needed.

As for the other strategies, my circumstances didn't give me the chance to utilise them, as I've been 'flying solo' for many years. However, I'm sure for those of you who are classified as a couple, I believe they may be more helpful than you think.

At least you should be made aware of them and give some thought to each of them.

Salary sacrificing into super can save tax and boost your retirement nest egg. Be sure to consider your options before diving in.

In closing, I would like you to take 10 minutes and sit down and have a look at a salary sacrificing calculator. Put your financial details into one of them. Perhaps you could start with ASIC's website www.moneysmart.gov.au and check out the Super Contributions Optimiser calculator. Then again click into any one of the calculators available on the internet and you will be surprised or shocked even with the results. Your own super fund may even have a calculator on their website that you can use.

There are a range of super and retirement calculators that can help you make informed decisions about your super.

If you are already salary sacrificing extra pre-tax contributions into your super, well done! For those of you who aren't, check with your employer if you are able to do so and if so, start salary sacrificing as soon as you can. It's never too late to boost your retirement savings.

To all those couples out there, set half an hour aside with a calendar entry in your phone and look at your options to either contribution splitting or whether it's viable for you to consider spouse contributions to your super. I'm sure you won't regret it.

My only wish is that I should have started salary sacrificing much sooner than I did. If I had, I would have been in an even better situation than I am today. Personally, I'm doing really well!

Chapter 8: The Common Denominator. It's YOU

'If you're in a household that has a passion for financial education, then you're much more likely to value it. Not only will you end up learning more about how to manage your money well, you'll also generate more wealth'—Mark Tanner, University of Queensland.

How Financially Literate Are Australians?

Did you know that fewer than half of all Australians could answer all five basic financial questions correctly from the questions below?

1. Suppose you put A$100 into a no-fee savings account, with a guaranteed interest rate of 2% per year. You don't make any further payments into this account and you don't withdraw any money. How much would be in the account at the end of the first year, once the interest payment is made?

2. Imagine now that the interest rate on your savings account was 1% per year and inflation was 2% per year. After one year, would you be able to buy more than today, the same as today, or less than today with the money in this account?

3. Do you think that the following statement is true or false? 'Buying shares in a single company usually provides a safer return than buying shares in a number of different companies.'

4. Again, please tell me whether you think the following statement is true or false: 'An investment with a high return is likely to be high risk.'

5. Suppose that by the year 2020 your income has doubled, but the prices of all the things you buy have also doubled. In 2020, will you be able to buy more than today, the same as today, or less than today with your income?

Of concern is the large gender gap in the results. While 50% of men managed to score a perfect five, only 35% of women did the same. That means 65% of women, or to put it into simpler terms, 65 women out of 100, couldn't answer the questions correctly. That's a huge difference in my opinion and hence the reason for my book.

This means that women generally are struggling to understand basic financial literacy. If they don't understand the above questions asked of them, what hope have they of knowing what to do with and understand superannuation, budgeting and debt consolidation, to name a few?

Professor Roger Wilkins of the Melbourne Institute of Applied Economic and Social Research, who is also the Deputy Director of the HILDA survey and it's this survey from which the questions above come from, is quoted as saying 'that the results weren't what he was expecting'. He goes on to say that 'he believes the gender divide is more likely a reflection of social and behavioural factors than any real differences in inherent abilities'. 'Men tend to take more of an interest in money matters, which might reflect traditional gender roles and norms more than anything else,' he says.

Chapter 8: The Common Denominator. It's YOU

Why Does It Matter?

The survey found low financial literacy usually translates to poor financial health. For example, poverty rates among the least financially literate are twice as high as the most literate group. Those with low financial literacy are also less likely to get involved in household budget decisions, have a lower tendency to save and are consequently more vulnerable to experiencing financial stress.

This is now coming to the surface as the rate of older women—those aged 55 and over— was the fastest-growing group of homeless Australians between 2011 and 2016, increasing by 31%. It is likely this trend will continue given the ongoing shortage of affordable housing, the ageing population, and the significant gap in wealth accumulation between men and women across their lifetimes.

These are alarming statistics and so it's for this reason we as women need to understand some basic financial literacy so that we can understand and look after our own financial well-being.

Funnily enough, another fact to come from the HILDA survey is that people who have the highest financial literacy seem to be those who are nearing retirement. Perhaps this is because people in this age group are more engaged with their superannuation funds, thus making them more focused on financial matters.

However, knowledge alone isn't enough to improve someone's financial health; it's about what you can do with that knowledge.

Understanding Your Own Financial Health

Have you ever thought about what your net worth is? By this I mean have you taken the time to write down what assets you have as a total amount minus any liabilities or debt you may have? It's important to maintain a positive net worth not only as it keeps you on a positive financial course, but it could help in times when maybe you want to borrow funds for a loan, saving you money over the long run. One of the first steps on your path to practical wealth is to calculate your net worth. This will give you a starting point to look back on over the coming months and years.

When crunching the numbers for your net worth, take the following steps:

1. **Note your assets.** Begin by adding up the current market value of your assets including your home, savings accounts, term deposits, any shares you may have or investment properties, valuable possessions such as jewellery and collectibles and cars, boats, those sorts of things. Even if it's a rough estimate, it will give you an idea.

2. **Note your liabilities.** Itemise all your financial liabilities or simply put, note down and add up what money you owe. This could be a mortgage, personal loan, car loan, student loan, credit card payments or anything you need to pay off. These days you may have Zip Pay and Ezi-Pay payments which are classified as liabilities. Virtually any money you have borrowed for whatever reason and needs to be paid back is a liability and considered as outstanding debt.

Chapter 8: The Common Denominator. It's YOU

As you total your liabilities, examine how much debt you are carrying now. While low debt levels are manageable, higher amounts may impact your long-term plans. Consider how paying down your debt could increase your ability to reach your goals.

3. **Subtract your total liabilities from your total assets.** This is your net worth.

Your net worth is a benchmark for gauging whether your assets are increasing over time. If you are moving in a positive direction, this is great.

If your net worth is only holding steady or declining, you'll want to identify the causes and take action. To streamline the process, set up a spreadsheet to track how you are going.

By doing this exercise every 6 – 12 months it can help you compare the figures with the previous year's calculations and measure progress. It is also an effective way to plan out your financial goals going forward.

Your Credit Score

I bet this is probably something many of you have never heard of. However, knowing your credit score could be very beneficial to you, particularly if you are wanting to borrow money for something, i.e. house purchase or motor vehicle.

Lenders use your credit score or credit rating as it is also known to decide whether to give you credit or loan you money. Your credit score is used to represent your credit worthiness, which translates into the likelihood that you'll pay your loan off in a timely manner.

If you don't know your credit score and you are knocked back for getting a loan, this could be the reason why the lender has rejected your application. Knowing what it is could help you in the long run.

Your credit score is based on personal and financial information about you that's kept in your credit report.

If managed wisely, it can bring you peace of mind. If not managed properly, it could restrict you from borrowing funds and therefore, delay your ability to reach your financial goals and result in you spending more money than necessary to make up for past mistakes.

You can receive your credit score for free. There are numerous websites, for example, Credit Savvy, Finder, GetCreditScore, which you can access and your credit score will usually be provided to you within minutes. As usual, avoid any provider that asks you to pay or wants your credit card details.

How Often Should You Check Your Credit Score?

A minimum of once a year to check for accuracy and any potential fraud attempts. If you've been a victim of identity theft, enrolling in some type of credit monitoring service may be best for your score and your peace of mind going forward.

Chapter 8: The Common Denominator. It's YOU

Tips for Having a Strong Credit Score

It's essential that you pay your bills on time. If you're late on a consistent basis, this will hurt your credit score. This doesn't just apply to credit cards. It considers other things such as your mortgage payments, loan repayments, etc.

Ensure Your Credit Card Is Carrying a Low or Zero Balance

Having maxed-out cards translates into a low amount of available credit (meaning lenders think you need to borrow funds to live day to day or you aren't tracking your spending closely) and this, therefore, lowers your score which is what you don't want.

Be proactive. If there's an issue that you foresee, such as being late on a payment, a bounced cheque or anything else for that matter, reach out to the company involved to give them a heads-up. You'll likely establish a better rapport with them and it will prevent them from having to track you down. You may even be able to get any fees associated with your situation waived.

Plan for the Unexpected

Make sure you are protected with the right kinds of insurance as well as having your estate plans in order.

Estate Planning

Even though it can be uncomfortable to think about your eventual passing, estate planning is an important topic to address in your financial review. Unfortunately, death is inevitable and I don't get why this subject is so taboo to discuss.

This is an area I'm quite passionate about, particularly from a financial point of view. When I was a financial planner, I would ask people if they had a will. Most people said no, which really astonished me. Having a will in place is more relevant to those of you who are in a relationship of some kind and have assets, especially a mortgage.

Think about your loved ones and the effects of having your wishes and specific requests documented and in place should they be confronted with the unexpected. Being organised and prepared will bring them a sense of comfort during what is usually a most stressful time. Make time to see a solicitor to put your will in place, any power of attorneys that may be needed, family trusts and guardianship provisions for children.

In addition, be sure to review and update any beneficiary information which may be required annually or as situations change, for example, divorce, marriage and children, to name a few.

When thinking about your need for a will, consider the following:

- How do you want your personal assets to be distributed?
- Who stands to inherit them?

Chapter 8: The Common Denominator. It's YOU

- Are there certain items or gifts that you would want to go to specific people? For example, your assets could pass on to your spouse, but you could indicate that your grandmother's jewellery be passed on to your sister or your DVD collection be donated to a local charity.

Creating a will allows you to appoint an executor of your estate and provides details on how your assets should be distributed in the event of your death.

Should you become incapacitated, who would you want to carry out any financial tasks on your behalf?

Do you own a business? Who would take care of it in the event of your death?

I mentioned earlier about having a power of attorney in place. This could be a spouse, sibling or parent to perform certain actions on your behalf, such as paying bills and making financial decisions, if you are unable to perform these tasks yourself.

In case of an medical emergency, who do you want responsible for making decisions on your behalf if you are unable to do so?

If you have young children, who do you want to care for them, should something happen to you and your partner? Without an approved legal guardian, which can be stated in your will or trust, any interested parties, ranging from family friends to relatives to social services agencies, may apply for guardianship through the courts.

Have there been any recent transitional changes in your life such as marriage, divorce, birth of a child or sickness?

It's important to ensure that all documents and designations remain aligned with your current situation and wishes.

Personal Insurance

I'm sure many of you don't think twice about insuring your car, home and contents. Some of you who may have rental properties even take out landlord insurance; however, the amount of people who don't have adequate insurance for themselves is to be questioned.

Odds are, if you are a woman, you're most likely to classify yourself as risk-averse, preferring to cover off all contingences— but you might be taking some significant risks without even realising it. What about your health and income? We have this attitude that 'nothing is going to happen to me'. However, we are not invincible and many of us don't consider the possibility of illness or injury and how either of these might affect our financial commitments and situation.

Let's be realistic and look at some probabilities of something going wrong: over a 35-year period, the chance of having your house and/or contents damaged or destroyed by fire is one in seven. Compare this with the odds of suffering a major medical trauma, such as cancer or heart disease, over the same time frame—age 30 to 65—and the likelihood is a sobering one in three.

Chapter 8: The Common Denominator. It's YOU

Consider the following statistics: one in two Australian women will suffer a major health trauma, such as a heart attack or cancer, before reaching the age of 70. The lifetime risk of suffering cancer is one in four for women and one in three for men. Breast cancer affects one in eleven women in Australia. We also have a one in three chance of being unable to work for at least three months due to sickness or injury—and 50% of those affected will still be unable to work after six months.

It's not until someone close to us is affected with a health issue or accident that the penny drops. I want you to at least look at what is on offer with regards to personal insurance. Not having some form of personal insurance in place, for example, income protection or trauma insurance, could put a huge strain on the family finances at a time of great emotional stress. Stress as we know plays a big part in most illnesses these days and an accident or injury can cause additional stress if you haven't got some measures in place to deal with the unexpected.

The ability to still be paid an income, to be able to pay for alternative medical treatment or take time out after a serious illness or injury can make all the difference to your recovery and your emotional well-being.

Action Steps for You to Do

1. If you are having trouble working out what's an asset and a liability, go to the link highlighted and use the net worth calculator https://moneysmart.gov.au/managing-debt/net-worth-calculator from the MoneySmart website and follow the prompts.

You could be in for a shock or a pleasant surprise, depending on your financial situation.

2. Take the time to go to one of the websites listed in the chapter with regards to getting your credit score, for example https://www.creditsavvy.com.au/. It will literally take five minutes and again, you will learn something that could prove quite valuable to you.

Chapter 9: Time to Take Control

'A big part of financial freedom is having your heart and mind free from worry about the what-ifs in life'—Suze Orman, financial planner, author and American TV host.

It's never too late to get started with working towards your financial goals. I didn't start thinking about my own financial well-being until I was in my early '40s, when I wrote down my first financial goal of wanting to be a millionaire. I always knew that if I put my mind to it and did certain things along the way, it would happen.

And after years of planning, budgeting, watching my spending habits and doing some of the other things I speak about in the previous chapters, I can honestly say that I did achieve my dream of becoming a millionaire and it was through property investment. I knew it would never be through being a secretary or wage earner.

Now with all that is going on in the world, I do have an emergency fund, I do still have one of my investment properties that has been mine for the last 25 years, I do have a better amount in my super than I did previously, thanks to the sale of one of my investment properties in July last year, and I do have a solid savings account to weather any possible storms or a change in my life's journey.

I didn't have much at all in my super when I decided that I'd had enough of 'herding cats' after 47 years of working full time. I had about $300,000 in my super. I would have had less if I didn't start salary sacrificing about five years before

I quit working and boy, do I wish I had done that sooner as well. This is pittance in the scheme of things.

Salary sacrificing wasn't something that I was familiar with until later in my working career. No one ever suggested it to me and it wasn't talked about where I worked. It was always my plan, or goal, if you like, to build a portfolio of investment properties worth a million dollars that would eventually be my way of building up my super balance before I reached pension age. I've done that and I'm still contributing to my super to this day.

And speaking of super, in 2018 the Association of Superannuation Funds of Australia (ASFA) calculated that a comfortable retirement for a single person requires a lump sum at retirement of approximately $545,000. For a couple, the equivalent lump sum is $640,000.

With those figures in mind, look at the chart below: it's some average super balances at different ages for men and women.

● 2017 – 18 average balances for men
● 2017 – 18 average balance for women

For Australians aged 25 to 34

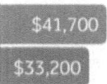

For Australians aged 35 to 44

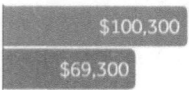

For Australians aged 45 to 54

$196,400
$129,100

For Australians aged 55 to 64

$332,700
$245,100

For Australians aged 65 to 74

$446,600
$378,600

For Australians aged 75 and over

$366,200
$270,300

For women in my age group, 55 – 64, the average super balance is $245,100 and yet when you look at the figures from ASFA and the pension age is 65, women are well below in their super at $545,000 to live comfortably. That's a gap of just under $300,000. That's a big difference and we are way behind in our super compared to males as the figures show and there are reasons for that as well, being broken working patterns, the gender pay gap and increasing casualisation of the workforce, to name a few.

We need to be more financially savvy. We need to start taking action and putting into place goals or plans for us now and in retirement, otherwise we are going to be another statistic of females being homeless in our late '50s, early '60s and older.

This is reality, particularly for those women who rent and don't own their own property.

I've done a lot of research on financial well-being for women and it seems from studies that I have read, they suggest that there is a direct correlation between a woman's personality characteristics and her financial habits. Assertiveness, openness to change and an optimistic outlook are the qualities that tend to lead to smart money choices.

They also say our problems with money are manifestations of problems in our lives and relationships. Work on the money issues and many of the other problems will take care of themselves; or work on the other problems and the money problems will take care of themselves.

For many people, money is an emotionally charged issue. It may represent power, or love, or control, especially in relationships. Our beliefs about money and our emotional attachments to it strongly influence the way we spend and handle money.

I'm a firm believer of this as I was always told that if you are in a relationship, the three things that stress people out is money, the in-laws and dying. Get your financial situation under control and you won't have to worry about your financial circumstances, you'll have money set aside for the inevitable and then you only have to get things worked out with the in-laws.

If you aren't where you should be, financially speaking, examine what drives you emotionally when it comes to money and try to figure out the psychological stumbling blocks that keep you from becoming financially independent.

Chapter 9: Time to Take Control

What Can We Do to Better Our Financial Future?

1. **Very important.** Don't rely on someone else, like a husband, boyfriend or partner for your financial security. Educate yourself about money management. I'm sure the book will enlighten you and give you some ideas to think about and put into action.

2. **Set goals.** Believe me, it is the key to my financial success and it will be yours.

3. **Don't use money to make yourself feel good.** My ex-husband used to give me $200 every time he went fishing. At the time, yes, it did feel good as I went and spent it on clothes and other things. In hindsight, I should have either saved it or said to him that I would rather he be here with me at the time or that we do something together with the money, like things that promote self-respect and creativity, so you don't have to seek those feelings through spending money. Another life lesson learnt at an early stage and one to remember.

4. **Spend less than you earn**—it's the secret to creating wealth. It's all about the 'ins' and 'outs'.

5. **Build an emergency fund.** Without one, losing your job or incurring a large, unexpected bill could force you to take on heavy credit card debt and could put you into a financial hole that will be difficult, if not impossible, to dig your way out of.

6. **Be involved in the day-to-day management of your family's finances and talk about money with**

your spouse. Communication is key to financial success when you're working towards it with a partner or spouse. Go ahead and block off times in your calendars to have monthly money meetings, where you can review your finances and ask important questions and make decisions together.

When you get married, the way you handle your finances will likely change. Though you should have discussed your personal finances, as well as financial goals for the future with your spouse before getting married, that doesn't always happen. That means there will probably be times when the two of you are at odds regarding your finances, either due to differing viewpoints on how to do things financially or perhaps even because you are financially incompatible.

That's when you should have a conversation with your spouse on the best way to formulate your budget, including how much money to allocate for groceries, eating out, clothing and other fun extras. Don't forget to set some money aside for starting your emergency fund, which is necessary for any workable budget. I also think it is a good idea to include a line item for money each spouse can spend, no questions asked. This can help keep your marriage healthy.

You should also agree on how to deal with other issues that may pop up, like an unexpected car or home repair, credit card debt or what to do if your parents ask for money. The last one particularly can often be the cause of many an argument when you've sat down to work out your budget. Take the time to listen to each other's reasoning of the pros and cons and hopefully after a sensible discussion on the subject, you should be able to resolve your differences.

7. **Think toward the future.** If one spouse simply does not see the need to worry about retirement or buying your first home, it can be frustrating for a spouse who's a planner, like me. Perhaps to curb this frustration and possible tension between the two of you, start by asking specific questions about the future, such as purchasing a house and saving for retirement. Often, if you can set goals together then it is easier to get the other spouse on board.

8. **Some people are not organisers or planners, but once they realise that the budget will help them reach their goals, they are more willing to work on a budget.** By illustrating how saving for the future will benefit them as well as yourself, you'll be able to get your reluctant partner on board with what you are trying to achieve.

9. **If you want to stop having financial fights with your partner, it's important to get on the same page.** Whether your primary financial goal is to pay down debt or stick to a realistic budget, it's important to communicate to your spouse what is important to you, money-wise. For example, you can explain how much value you put on his or her willingness to work on a budget. Alternately, be sure you know your

partner's financial goals and make working towards them a priority, as well.

10. **Be careful not to turn discussions about the budget into nagging sessions or start throwing accusations at each other about money.**

11. **Make accountability a priority.** One of the key things to managing money without fighting is to be on the same page with your budget and other financial goals. That means you'll need a way to have accountability, both to your budget and to each other. Once you're on the same page, you may be surprised at how much more smoothly your finances work—and how much more easily you and your spouse can discuss all things related to money.

12. **Don't take on your partner's or spouse's debt when you marry.** Perhaps you should protect yourself with a pre-nuptial agreement. They're not only for the rich. Some people may not agree with me on this one; however, I've worked very hard and smart at the same time to get to where I am financially. For me to get involved with someone and then be foolish enough to take on their debt, I would have to have rocks in my head. Better still, sit down and work out together how that person can get rid of their debt, rather than expecting you to take it on. You may not be in a good financial head space and situation yourself, so why make it doubly worse.

13. **Learn from your money mistakes.** Don't let them hobble you.

14. **Treat yourself.** After all this hard work, make room in your budget for small treats every now and then. It could be as simple as buying a cake from your favourite bakery or you might want to pamper yourself a little more with something like a massage. It's important to prioritise your savings. However, you also need to make some space for the fun stuff too.

15. **Lastly, get your estate plan in order.** Yes, you do need one as an estate plan protects your stuff, your assets and more importantly, your loved ones should something happen to you. Start the process of setting up these important legal documents. Your local solicitor should be able to help you with this.

Reaching financial goals is hard work. If you feel exhausted just thinking about all your to-dos to reach your financial milestones, find ways to keep your motivation high. Creating a vision board made up of your list of goals and placing them on the fridge or somewhere else where you will see it on a daily basis will remind yourself of what you are working towards each and every day. It's terrific for keeping your dreams alive.

Be in charge and set up that budget. Look at debt management and consolidation. Consider what type of spender you are.

This may seem like a lot to do, but just get started by doing at least one step. It may be starting a budget, sitting down and talking about your financial goals, curbing your spending habits or how to save more money.

When it comes to tackling your finances, understanding your goals, your cash flow and where your money is going is a great place to begin to get clarity on your path to financial success.

Understanding your own financial position to help you achieve your financial goals is dependent on your attitudes and beliefs about money and your willingness to take your financial future into your own hands.

Think of yourself one year from now. Maybe even write yourself a note and put it somewhere safe and note it in your calendar one year out. What do you want to say to the future you and what changes are you willing to make now, so that future you is in a better place? I can tell you from experience, change isn't easy, but it's worth it. Gaining control of your own financial well-being and the underlying emotional causes will be the best investment you'll ever make.

Chapter 10: Case Studies

Case Study no.1

Margaret was a stay-at-home mum until the '90s when she felt the need to get out into the workforce and earn some money for herself and her family. At first, Margaret took on part-time work in a deli until she found a full-time position in a bank. Her skill sets grew and Margaret continued working until she finally decided it was time to call it quits in 2017 and stepped away from the workforce.

As Margaret started working in the '90s, her superannuation balance at retirement age wasn't going to be substantial enough for her to retire comfortably. She had entered the workforce when superannuation had only just been introduced, and even whilst 'salary sacrificing' in her last permanent role, Margaret's final super balance was about $80,000.

At the age of 64, after 30-plus years of marriage, Margaret got divorced in 2017.

The divorce meant that Margaret was entitled to half the proceeds from the sale of the marital home and an amount they shared from their bank savings account.

The divorce proceeds were put into Margaret's superannuation account which did bump up the balance. However, with property prices the way they are now, if Margaret was to use that money to buy a place to put a roof over her head, pretty much of what's in her super account would be taken to buy something. Margaret would virtually have nothing left over, only her savings, and that's not a huge amount. Her only option then would be to rent.

Circumstances change and Margaret moves interstate to take up the role as carer for her elderly father in his home that also belongs to her brother. With careful planning and considering all her options, it's decided that the huge garage at the property where Margaret lives is capable of being fitted out to accommodate Margaret where she can live quite comfortably down the track when her time as carer to her father ceases.

Even though Margaret's super balance is under $500,000, while not substantial by any means, it is better than nothing.

Fortunately for Margaret, things could have been much worse. With planning and consistently looking at ways to enhance and grow her super, Margaret is in a happy place.

Case Study no.2

Marie's story is one of resilience and determination and for the most part she has endured hardship, both personally and financially. At eighteen years of age, having come from a simple background of not having much in the way of material things like money and bought clothes, she meets the love of her life and gets married.

It's 1973; there's no superannuation at this stage and the married couple are both working. They decide that they would live off one wage and save the other towards a home deposit. It's been the Aussie dream to one day own your own home and even back in the '70s, it was something that each married couple strived for.

Chapter 10: Case Studies

Two years pass and in 1975 they finally have a deposit for a home loan. They decide to buy a house for $32,000 in Bundoora in Melbourne. It's at this stage where Marie sits down and puts together a family budget by adding up all the bills she has received over 12 months. From there she takes it even further and divides it by 26 weeks to work out fortnightly payments as there is only one income each fortnight. Larger items like carpet, window furnishings and white goods were purchased on interest-free terms and smaller items on layby.

Back in those days, layby (which I also used and was known as the layby queen) was a system whereby you would pay a deposit on the goods to hold them for a given period. It was generally three months, although it depended on what you were buying, where you bought it and the value of the goods.

These items would be held by the company you bought it from and generally each week, you would go back to the store and pay some more money off your layby. Once you had made the final payment and owed nothing, you were then able to take the goods home.

You could say that layby back then was like what is used these days, like Ezi-Pay and Afterpay, although I think you can take the goods with you even though you haven't finished paying for them. Back then until you paid that final amount, the goods were stored for you in the organisation's warehouse area.

In 1976, Marie has her first child and tackles the family budget once again as she has always been frugal with her finances. There's a mortgage that needs to be paid and the bills keep coming. With only one wage still going into the household finances and three people now to feed and clothe, she needs to be.

Marie was a great advocate for budgeting. She would literally sit down each week and budget for that week. She would search the supermarkets' catalogues and buy what she needed that was 'on special'. Once her grocery list was sorted, her next task was to work out how much was needed to be put aside for bills and the various insurances that the couple held, like house, car and contents insurance. Every cent was religiously accounted for.

In 1979, Marie has her second child. Her budgeting routine needs to be completely revised and refreshed as she needs to work out how the household finances are going to be managed now that there's another mouth to feed. Marie now diligently phones each provider of insurance and those companies where her payments are made on a yearly basis so that she can save money by reducing the premiums. Money needs to be saved and all avenues are explored.

In 1982 the couple put their Bundoora home on the market and decide to move to Macedon. Along comes 1983 and Macedon is impacted by the Ash Wednesday bushfires. Although the house where they were living wasn't burnt, they decided to move to Keilor Downs because of restrictions with only having one car for the whole family.

Marie's finances were going in all directions at this time, so her budgeting prowess was put to the test again. Still not to be deterred, she managed the family's finances with dedication and efficiency.

Chapter 10: Case Studies

Her third child is born and it's 1985.

Four years on and Marie's husband is offered a job in Tasmania. The family of five uproot and move to Tassie. Properties are bought and sold and the family's financial situation is looking grim.

It doesn't matter how much Marie works out her budget each week, it's decided that Marie needs to find a job. The 'stay-at-home mum' leaves her young family to begin working. For 16 years Marie has managed her household finances on one wage which has been a mammoth task and up to this stage has done rather well, all things considered.

In 1990, the 'recession that we had to have' hits the family when the business agreement that Marie's then-husband had entered into with the move to Tassie goes belly up and after much effort to resurrect their situation, it's decided to cut their losses and declare bankruptcy. This at any time is a massive decision to undertake and at this stage of Marie's life it's huge. She loses her car, the family home, and the marriage is put under a huge strain.

A fresh start is needed so the family move back to Melbourne to be with her parents and where the family now live until things get sorted. Marie eventually finds a rental property big enough for the family and shortly afterwards, secures employment. Her two older children have part-time jobs and helps their mother financially.

Finally, it's all too much and Marie separates from her mentally abusive and alcoholic husband in 2001.

Her budgeting skills are at it again. Over time she manages to save enough money to buy a car. Nothing fancy, but it takes Marie and her family from place to place.

The next 15 years, there would be times when Marie had three to four part-time jobs, working 50 – 60 hours a week for not big wages. As she manages her time with her children, she also manages the household finances again. Looking for those elusive specials at the supermarket and anywhere else that she can save money.

These last few years, Marie has had health issues which required major surgery. She now works at one job which is part time. Her children are adults with children of their own.

And Marie still manages her finances like clockwork. Her budget now is worked out monthly as that is how she is paid. But it's worked out to the last cent. Her grocery money is put aside for each month, her tax return is used to pay off large expenses like her health insurance which she pays in advance and yearly. By doing this Marie saves about three hundred dollars a year and over time these amounts soon add up and can be used somewhere else within Marie's budget.

Throughout Marie's journey she has managed to get by with being frugal with what money she has had during her life and has certainly lived within her means. She has had to, otherwise Marie would certainly be another statistic for homeless women in this age group in Australia as she owns no property.

Her superannuation balance is not huge by any means and she is close to receiving the Age Pension. Marie now lives in my granny flat in my mother's backyard and is there for my mother who is elderly and needs help from time to time, which I am eternally grateful for.

Marie has sacrificed a lot during her life. Her words of advice are to keep on top of your finances all the time and to make sure you check your credit card statement every month.

Case Study no.3

At the age of 31, while still single, Mary set herself a personal financial goal that she wanted to be debt free at 45. Mary didn't have a written plan for her spending, nor did she budget per se; however, she always managed her finances from week to week. She would put money aside for her bills, then put a small amount into a savings account and what was left over was for Mary to spend.

Mary was made redundant from her employment twice in her working life. The first time it occurred in 1987, instead of splurging the proceeds, she wisely invested it. Now that money was working for her and it was locked away for a couple of years.

In 1990 Mary decided to buy a two-bedroom unit in Altona in Melbourne for $112,000. At the time Mary borrowed about $89,000 for her home loan. Mary promptly set up fortnightly repayments to pay off her mortgage quicker and always put any extra money she had left over from her weekly wage on her mortgage payments. By doing this Mary was cutting years off the time the loan was set for (usually about twenty-five years) as well as paying less interest over the life of her loan. A win-win situation.

Mary did have a credit card with $1,000 limit but she never bought things on credit. It was there to have in case of an emergency.

Several years later, Mary was made redundant for the second time. Again, Mary could have been silly and spent what money she had received from her redundancy payout. Instead the money was used to pay the balance of her home loan.

When Mary turned 56 she realised she wasn't going to have a huge superannuation balance either by the time she retired, so she decided that she should start to salary sacrifice while she was still working full time. And today, five years on, Mary is still salary sacrificing within her fortnightly pay to boost her superannuation balance as she nears retirement age.

Mary was never one to miss out on doing things with her friends when she was single. If she was asked out to dinner and couldn't afford to spend money on dinner that week, she would still meet her friends and have an entrée with them instead of a large meal. Or catch up with them over the occasional drink afterwards.

Fast forward and Mary is now in a relationship and has been for 14 years. She has a reasonable amount of money in her super, has paid her home loan off, has done some renovations to her unit which have also been paid for and now works four days a week.

Her motto is 'be sensible with your money, don't spend what you don't have' and is a firm believer of living within your means. And her final message is 'don't spend what you can't pay for'.

Good advice from someone who has thought about her financial well-being as she heads into retirement. She has set herself up well from her early days of sacrificing that dinner with friends that she couldn't afford that week to buying unnecessary things.

Case Study no.4

Many years ago, my parents, who were in their '60s at the time, started thinking about how they were going to maximise what money they had saved over the years and what Dad would do with his money once he retired from the workforce. Yes, even back then, once people got near retirement age, they started considering all their options on how they could make their life better and be more financially sound.

Bear in mind, my parents went through the Great Depression of the 1930s. During this time, Australia suffered years of high unemployment, poverty, plunging incomes and lost opportunities for personal advancement.

Thankfully my father was always employed during this time; however, wages were low in the scheme of things. Dad was the breadwinner and Mum stayed home doing the household chores and looking after myself and my sister.

When I think back, my mother was fantastic with financial literacy. She paid all the bills, put money aside each week for this and that—that must have been where I got my skills from—and kept an eye on the bank account. If she wanted something that wasn't included in the weekly budget, she would save for it or put it on layby.

If I remember at the time, I was looking at my own superannuation account and was given the name of a financial planner who they knew and recommended that I could talk to about this and that.

My father was very risk-averse. Perhaps it had something to do with Mum knowing all the financial stuff and Dad wasn't involved and therefore, he didn't understand how it all worked. It took him months to save and get the deposit for a block of land in Glenroy, where my father eventually built the family home, so he was very unsure of speaking to a financial planner and being told what to do with his money when he retired.

Anyway, I finally convinced my father to at least speak to the financial planner to see what he had to say. He had some very sound advice and put into simple terms what he thought my father should do with his money.

Well, fast forward 30-odd years and my mother is now living very comfortably after Dad took the time to listen to someone with financial expertise and with Mum's basic understanding of what was being proposed, they accepted the advice. It was the best thing they could have done. I guess I also had something to do with it, as it was me who made them see some sense in being financially savvy and aware of their financial well-being when Dad was fully retired.

The moral of the story here is that you don't need a financial planner, although it did help in this instance. In my parents' case the information received was invaluable, but it's more to do with taking the time to sit down and think and talk about your options, do your planning, have that budget in place and research what is out there.

Chapter 10: Case Studies

Had my father not taken this advice, there is no way my mother would be in the financial situation she is in now and she is in her late 80s. Think of the consequences and plan for it accordingly.

Your Resources Compliments from Retirement Ready

Offer 1 – Free Budget Buster Template

Now more than ever, particularly since we have experienced changing times due to COVID-19, to help you get organised, I've created a budget template to get you started putting pen to paper and working out a budget for your own financial situation.

To get this budget template, email helen@beretirementready.com.au and it will be sent to you for free.

Offer 2 - Bust Your Money Fears Complimentary Sessions

Helen knows that not everyone's financial situation is the same. Most people hate talking about money and the problems associated with it. It is only through her own life experiences and since obtaining her financial planning qualifications—that has enlightened her and provided her with some valuable knowledge and advice—that she is happy to share it with people.

To get some clarity on your money boundaries, Helen is offering a free 30-minute conversation with her to help bust your money fears. Check in with her to discuss how she can help with allaying your worries on reining in your spending habits, putting pen to paper and doing a budget, or thinking that you can't do it, when you actually can when you have the know-how.

On offer each week are five sessions of a 30-minute conversation with Helen.

To receive this free offer, and it's only limited to five people per week, email helen@beretirementready.com.au to schedule a date and time with her.

Offer 3 – Conference Speaking Services

For the past seven years Helen Williams has been sharing her experiences on being Retirement Ready and now, more than ever, everyone over the age of 50 needs to increase their financial knowledge.

Increasingly she has become concerned with just how financially fit people are and is therefore drawn to the cause of enlightening and assisting people to better their financial situation. Helen believes that her purpose is to help people be more financially savvy and delivers her easy-to-understand content in a humorous, down-to-earth and engaging way.

Helen can speak on topics such as:

Positive Money Mindset –
Learn how to make money your friend
Super Made Simple –
Get back in control of your retirement
Easy Budget Breakthrough –
Make your money fit your lifestyle

Presentations can be customised for each event and are usually for a duration of 30-90 minutes. Contact Helen for availability and pricing.

To engage Helen to speak at your event,
email helen@beretirementready.com.au and submit an enquiry.

Note:
Any not-for-profits wishing to engage Helen to speak at their events, please be advised that these sessions will be free of charge.

Notes

Notes

Notes

Notes

www.ingramcontent.com/pod-product-compliance
Lightning Source LLC
Chambersburg PA
CBHW021152080526
44588CB00008B/307